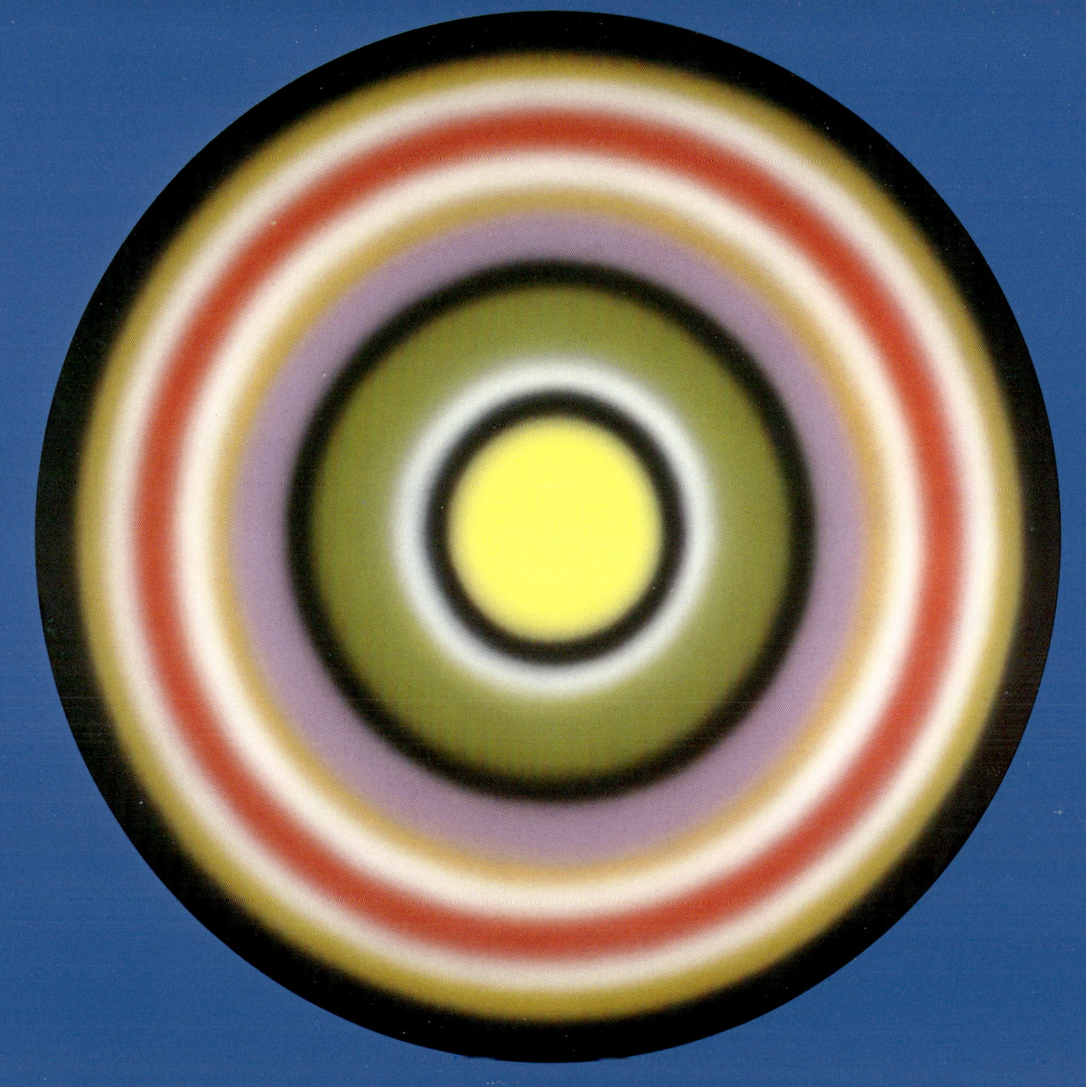

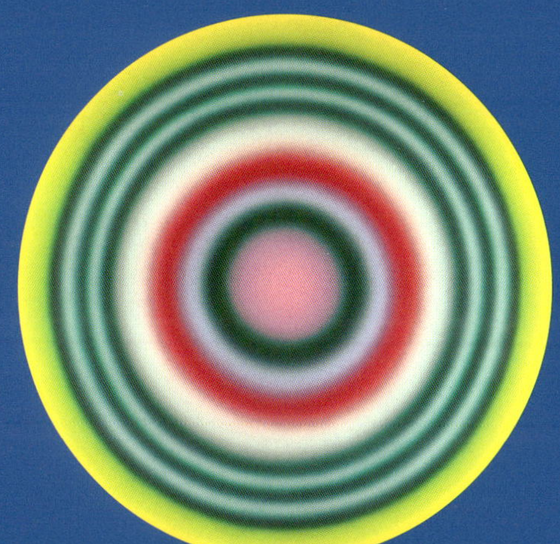

AF479260

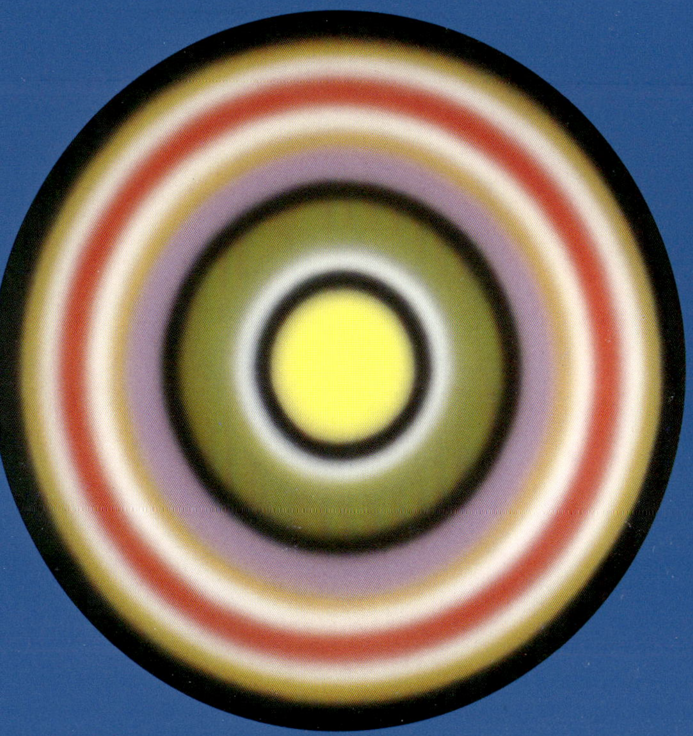

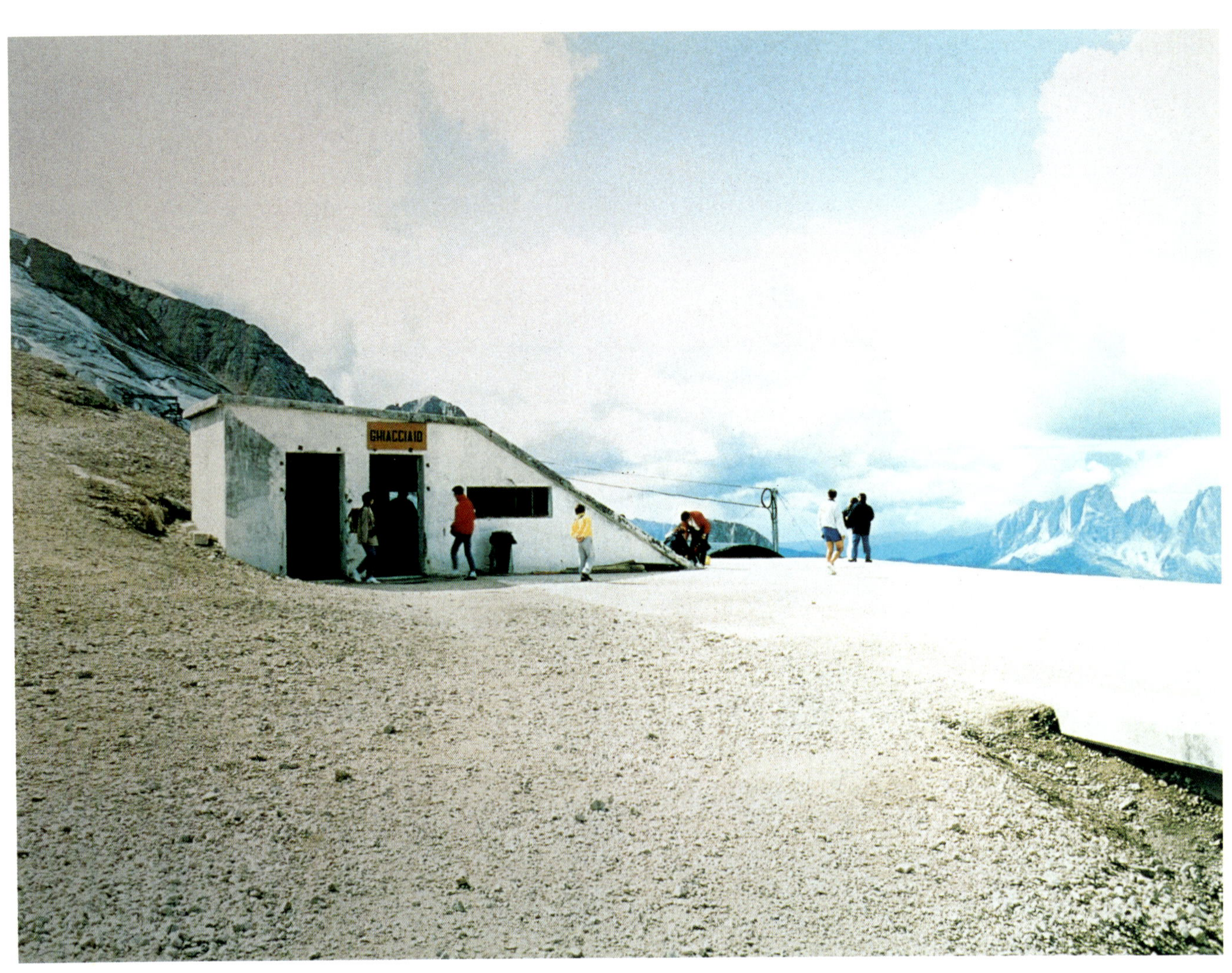
GHIACCIAIO

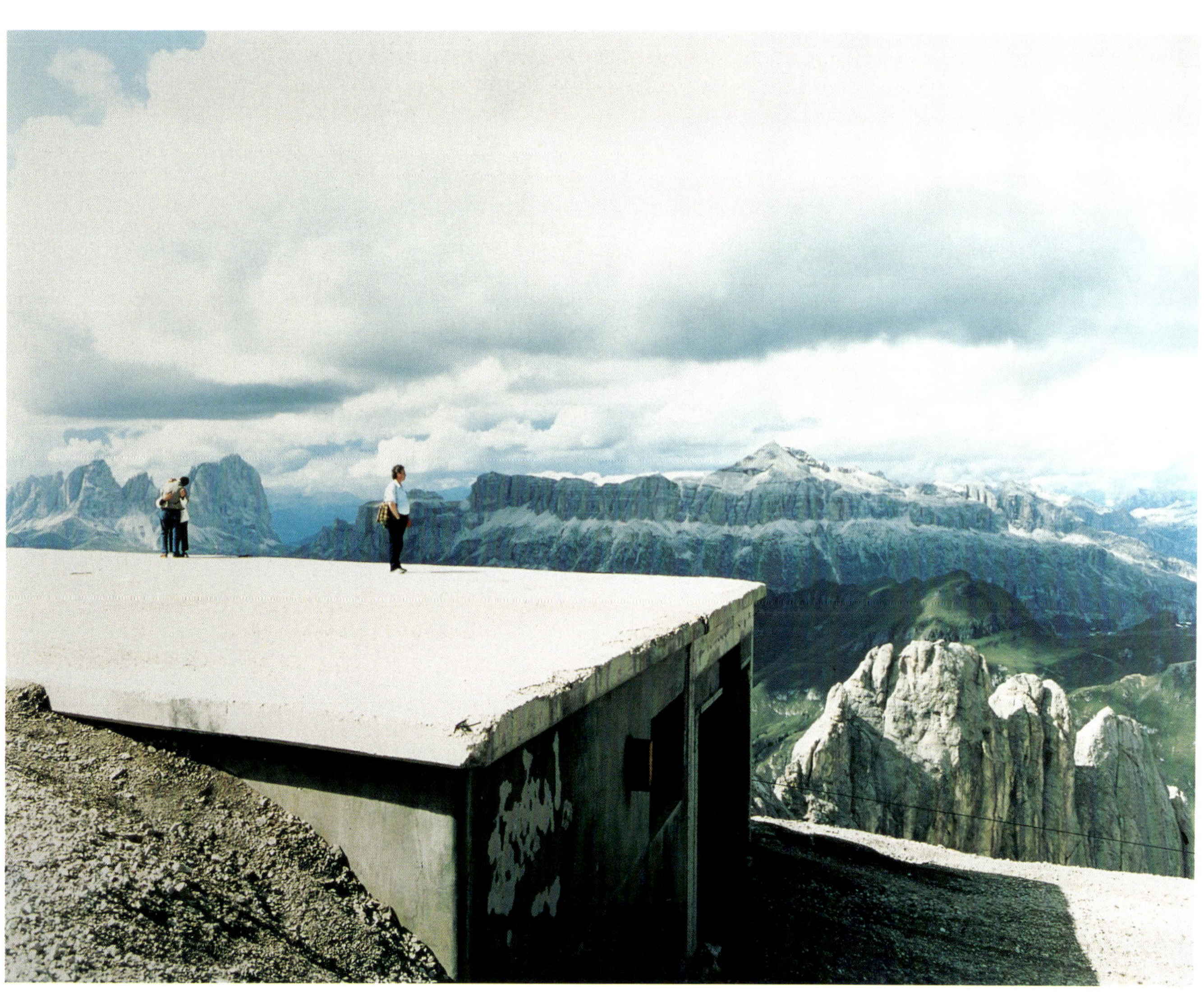

Designed and published in 1998 by The Saatchi Gallery
98A Boundary Road London NW8 0RH

Text © Patricia Ellis

Front cover:
Juan Uslé *Mal de Sol* 1999 (detail)
Rineke Dijkstra *Kolobrzreg, Poland, July 26, 1992*
     Dubrovnik, Croatia, July 13, 1996
     De Panne, Belgium, August 7, 1992
     Coney Island, N.Y., USA, June 20, 1993
     Hilton Head Island, S.C. June 24, 1992
Ugo Rondinone *No.90* 1997
Previous page: Walter Niedermayr *Marmolada Rifugio Serauta* (2 parts) 1992-93
colour photograph overall 103 x 262 cm
Overleaf: Giuseppe Gabellone *Untitled* 1997 photographic print 150 x 217 cm
Still from *Now Voyager* courtesy of Warner Brothers

Printed by The Pale Green Press
Printed and bound in Great Britain

ISBN 0 9527 453 99

EUROVISION

essay by Patricia Ellis

The Saatchi Gallery

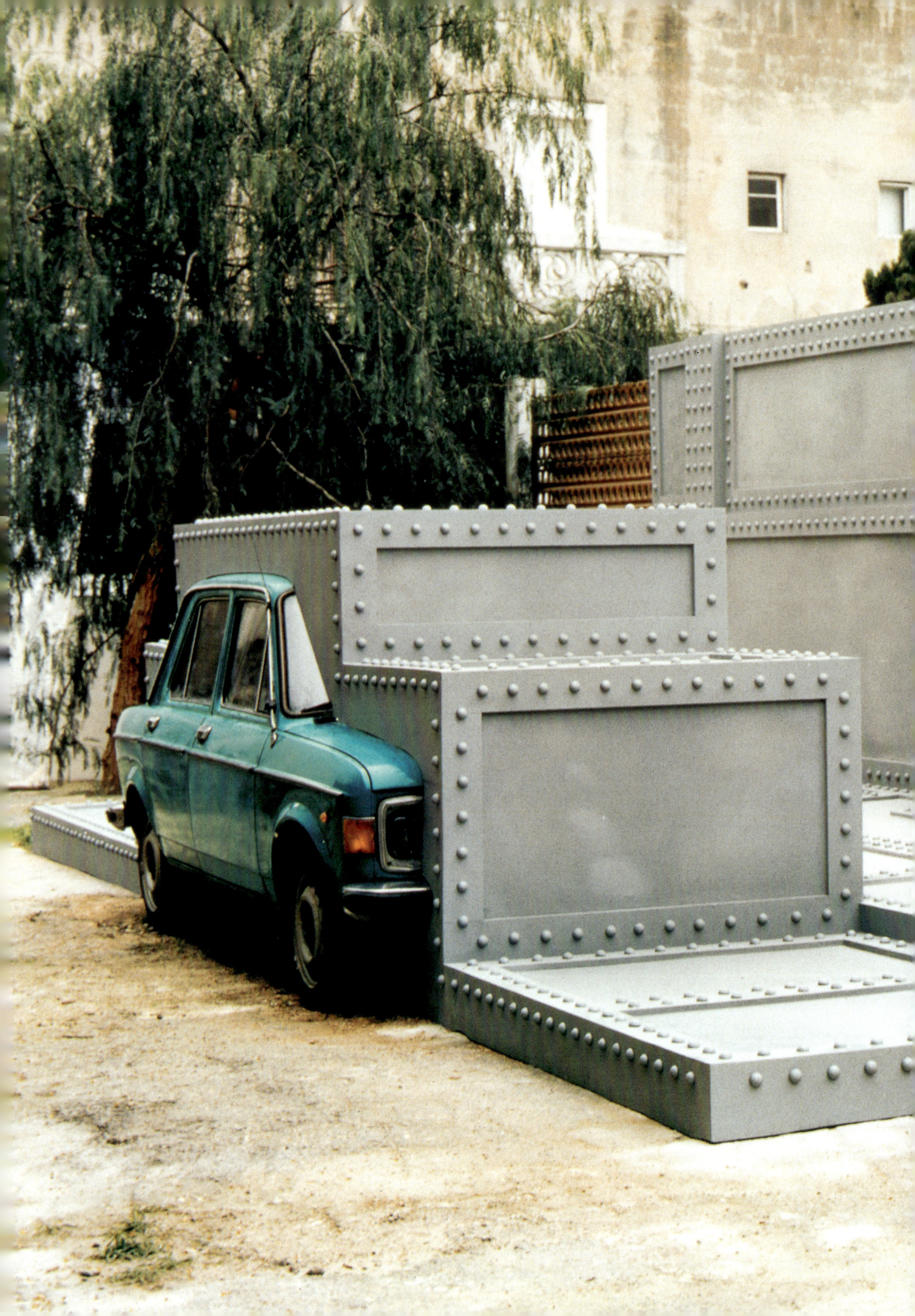

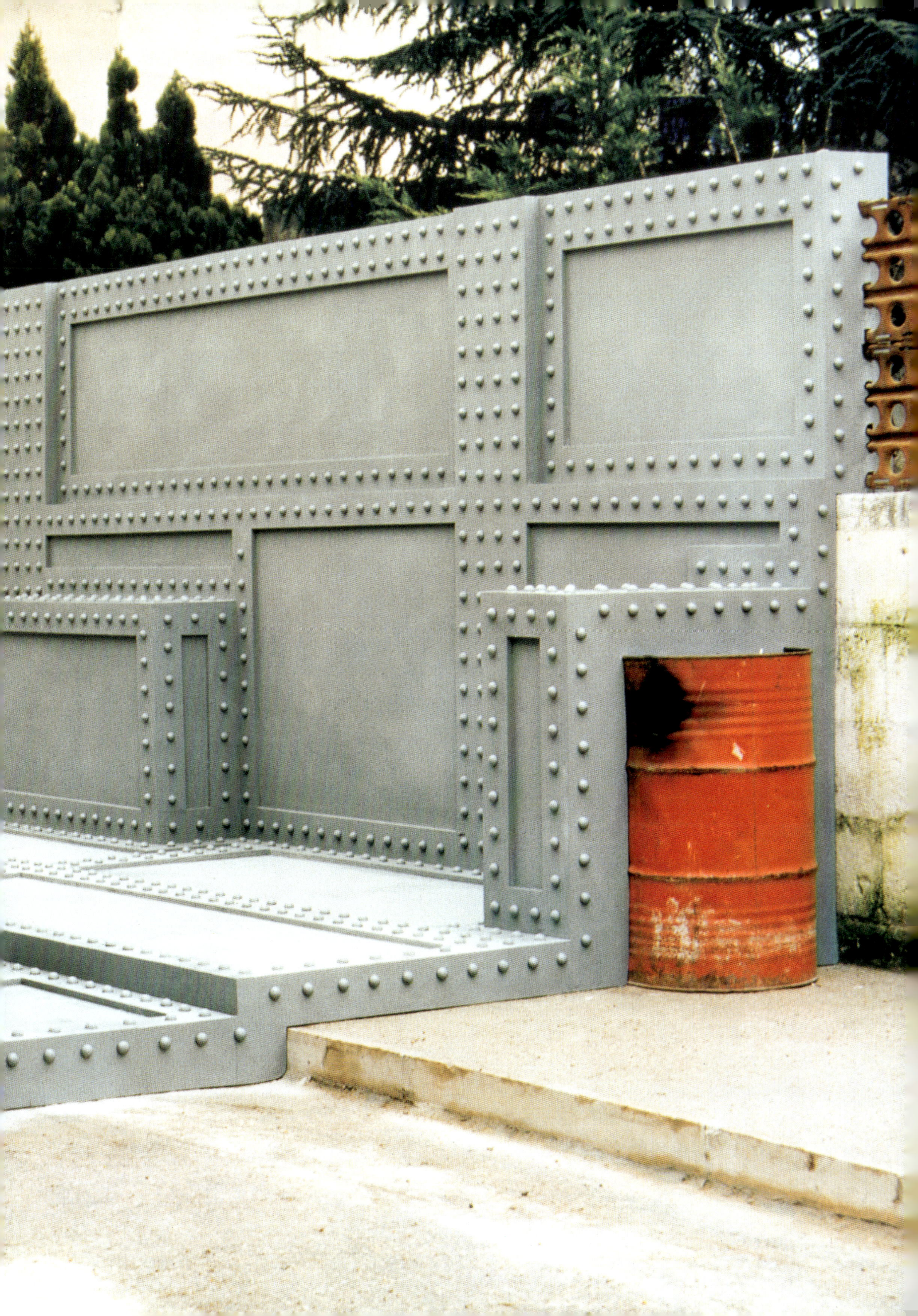

thomas **demand**

rineke **dijkstra**

EUROvISION

esko **männikkö**

ugo **rondinone**

juan **uslé**

The Saatchi Gallery

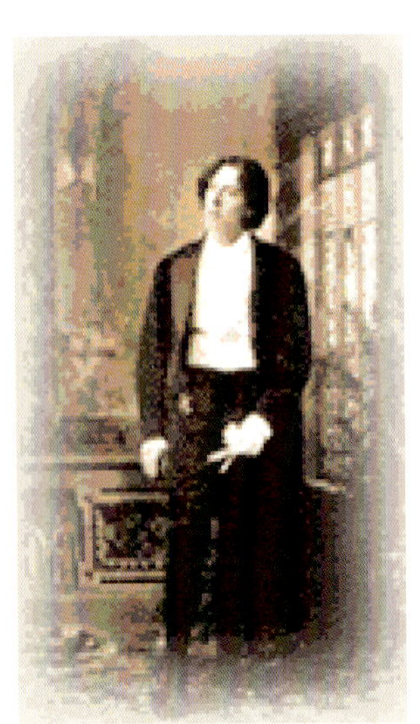

EUropium[1]

When one is in love, one always begins by deceiving oneself, and one always ends by deceiving others. That is what the world calls a romance.[2]

Europe practically *invented* Romance. Knights, Princesses, Dragons; Love and Chivalry and Adventure. Today romance still is being fanciful, chimerical in the face of adversity; Fantastic in the everyday. Sort of like deception, romance is *believing*. It's a little bit like falling in love.

Everybody's Smitten: Tales of European passion are found throughout contemporary lore[3], propagated/sustained by New World desire. Fuelled by plastic memories, this is a collective fabrication: a stereotyped continent of tulips and wooden shoes, matadors, berets, Autobahn, Moulin Rouge, double-decker buses and chintz decor. The sweet Mediterranean air thick with tobacco and cheese and perfume; This is the Europe of young lovers and timeless sophistication.[4] The slick, *á la mode* package of the newly abbreviated EU also intrigues: riddled with palimpsest secrets of richly emprised history. It is fantasy of enigma, fiction, fashion, power. It is a Europe-propelled illusion: Versace, Diana, Porsche, *La Femme Nikita, Pâté de foie Gras*. Superior in lifestyle, technology, celebrity: Europe is the ultimate desire.[5]

And very desirable indeed: This collection of European artists is *très* cosmopolitan. Hailing from Finland, Holland, Switzerland, Germany, and Spain[6] these artists draw from eclectic cultural, regional and artistic influence. Well into the age of Globalisation, there is nothing to distinctly mark these artists as being anything but *Worldly*. For them the idea of romance and Europe is manifest in the form of the international perception: these artists are perpetuating our fantasy.

As for the rest of us: we are being flirted with, charmed. Glamorising the everyday, sensationalising the defective, the work we are about to see weaves the most enchanting romance. Within these fictive pools it is left to us to dip below the surface.

This is a seduction; This is (maybe) a love story.

---

[1] The 50th Element (EU) of the Periodic Table: The screen of a colour-television tube is treated with Europium, which, when bombarded with electrons, produces the colour red. *(Funk and Wagnall's Encyclopaedia. Infopedia. USA: Softkey CD-ROM, 1996. Europium.)*

[2] *Oscar Wilde , The Picture of Dorian Gray. Merriam-Webster Dictionary of Quotations. Infopedia. USA: Softkey CD-ROM, 1996.*

[3] As a Canadian living in Britain, I'm neither American or European, so I apologise in advance for any generalised cultural mis-conceptions. I hope I'm using fairly well known illustrations which everyone can relate to, albeit most of them will be American, as I am anglophone and these references seem to be the most widely available.

[3] A recent portrayal of this contemporary myth in American media are the episodes of **Beverly Hills 90210** when Brenda and Donna go to Paris for the summer. They take up smoking, eat brains in a fancy restaurant and shop for *haute couture*, all the while speaking the perfect accent-less French they acquired in 4 years flat at Beverly High. Brenda eventually seduces an American boy by using a phoney French accent proving once and for all that European women *are* infinitely more exotic than Americans, even if they are Shannon Doherty. (FYI: This boy went on to portray Superman in the popular series **Lois and Clark**.)

[5] Europe is used to sell almost anything in America - The Scandinavian purity of New Jersey produced Häagan-Dazs, the European *chic* of former cosmetic clerk, Estée Lauder, the authentic Alpine comfort of Swiss Miss.

[6] Esko Männikkö is Finnish; Rineke Djikstra, Dutch; Ugo Rondinone, Swiss; Thomas Demand is from Germany; and Juan Uslé is from Spain (although he now lives in New York).

Esko Männikkö's photographs of the rural inhabitants of Northern Finland offer sensitive and personal insights to the roughness of arctic life. Inserted into weathered second-hand frames, these photographs become a provocative mixture of personal memoirs and (folk) art. This is an insider's view of a Europe thought only to be existing in fairy tales…

> **_Utajärvi:_** After a brisk morning ski, the old clock-maker retreats to his cabin. Sprawled like a teenager, he listens to his ghetto blaster, his headphones insulate his dreams. Amidst the magical protection of his treasures, his clocks weave a timeless spell: it's believable this workshop is enchanted.

This is the world of Esko Männikkö. A native of this region, he shares the experience of his subjects. Before taking these photographs, Männikkö lives with these people, working, eating, drinking, sharing: These are not documentary images, these are portraits of Männikkö's friends.

Romanticised in the minds of urbanites through a million unremembered homespun legends, these isolated European communities seem ancient. Männikkö's photographs tell the tale of the last bastion of European folk culture. Living in relative isolation almost void of outside influence, Männikkö's comrades offer kindly, humorous views of stylite culture and bonding. In these regions, self-consciousness seems obsolete: honesty overcomes embarrassment. We laugh enviously for their sincerity, in awe of their exoticism.

Breaking convention, we find ourselves confronted with glimpsing intimate scenes: a leathery farmer nurses a wee lamb in his kitchen; an intellectual sits with his books in his (almost) *nouveau chic* apartment. A woodland princess gives Disney-like audience to necrotic animals. A middle-aged man drapes a tapestry of a stag above a too-small single bed. In a moment of inspiration, an artist paints a brutish rainbow across the facade of his trading post.

These are not depictions of the triumph of spirit seen in the nostalgia of Rockwell, the frankness of Walker Evans or the jolly communities of Pieter Bruegel Sr. Männikkö's subjects are not bravely seeking rural dignity. Living in the North is their way of life: it is a way of choice, a way of conservation. And also disintegration. These still waters run much deeper.

Reality beneath the romance: Rineke Dijkstra's photo portraits of sexually aware bathing-suit clad teens and naked labour-scarred new mums lay bare topics of taboo. Within is a tenderness more poetic than myth...

Following in the genre of the great American traditions of Gidget[7], Annette and Frankie[8], and yes, even our contemporary Walsh's[9], Rineke Dijkstra's studies of teenagers on the beach bring to consideration the secret world of adolescence.

___Hilton Head Island, S.C., USA, June 24, 1992___ : A will-be buxom blond poses innocently against the Atlantic. She is bronzed and healthy, beautiful in her own mind as assured on TV. Though she is groomed for sex, she has no idea of what it actually means. She is a kitten because she is supposed to be, because all girls are. Her heart probably belongs to a boy in the ninth grade who doesn't even notice.

___Kolobrzeg, Poland, July 26, 1992 :___ The girl in the ill-fitting green bathing suit is the absolute epitome of beauty. She is sunken eyed, malnourished, thin lipped and gangly. In her unconsciously seductive pose she is all knobby joints and bony hips; she has two small bruises on her left leg. She is confident and fragile, tough and timid; she looks at you and it is absolutely personal.

The beauty of Botticelli's *Venus* tinged with the uncertainty of Edvard Munch's *Puberty* is combined in these youthful divas. Classically posed where the surf meets the sand, the reference to the Sea Nymph is made all the more hysterical[10] by the youths' awkward physique, and some how all the more tragic by the viewer's knowing and self-reflective indulgence.

Teenage sexuality has consistently been neatly skirted in the main stream; Focusing on wholesome coming of age has been a tidy way of ësterilising' this difficult stage. Depictions of pretty girls with frosty pink lipstick and robust, sporty boys have become iconographic mainstays of Mum and Dad approved Morality. Dijkstra, however, rejoices in their painstaking maladroitness, providing a counter-mythology to Elvis-ified beach nostalgia. She doesn't discredit romantic teenage ideology, she offers a different one: Her photographs are *Sexy[11]*.

They *are* Sexy - unchoreographed, un-enhanced, these teens are aware of their sexuality, they wear it cautiously and artlessly, their naiveté is part of the charm. They are unattractive,

---

[7] Originally starring pre-Oscar Sally Field, __Gidget__ won the hearts of 60's American TV lovers while she hung out on the beach with her friends.

[8] Post-Mickey-Mouse-Club/Pre-Skippy-Peanut-Butter-Ad Annette Funicello became the quintessential surfing icon of the 60s with her on screen shorter-in-real-life-than-you'd-think boyfriend: Real-life pop sensation Frankie Avalon. Check out: __Beach Blanket Bingo__ **(1965),** __Bikini Beach__ **(1964),** __Muscle Beach Party__ **(1964)** and __Hullabaloo__ **V.5 (1964).**

[9] Oh come on, get with it - 90210!

[10] This could be read as hysterical funny, or hysterical radical, depending on your disposition. If you don't know whether to laugh or cry, or maybe want to do both at the same time, you're probably feeling the right thing.

[11] OK, so everyone on earth has disagreed with me on this! But I stand by my observation - they ARE sexy. Maybe (hopefully) not to us, maybe not to each other, but in their own minds. Didn't you think you were sexy when you were 14? Didn't you desperately hope someone else would one day think so?

unprovacative and above all, unapologetic. These teens are crude, contemporary, fragile and oddly exotic compared to the domestic complacency and moral gushiness of the idealised California set[12]. Paradoxically real and romantic, sensual and clumsy. This is the anomaly of adolescence.

Grown up: Dijkstra's hard and truthful versions of Madonna and Child immediately shatter conventional romantic ideas of childbirth. The model of the New Mother is a cheerful size 10 reclined on crisp white sheets, surrounded by flowers, cuddling the new arrival. The popular image of the baby is a chubby six month old with a full head of hair. Comparatively, the beet-red wrinkled darlings in Dijkstra's pictures almost rival the mini-adult freakishness of painted Renaissance babies.

> ***<u>Tecla, Amsterdam, Netherlands, May 16, 1994:</u>*** Tecla stands looking timidly, defensively, pleadingly to the camera: She is shell-shocked, her body ravaged by the trauma of delivery, her mind overwhelmed by the enormity of it all. She clutches her baby awkwardly to her breast; a trickle of blood runs down her leg. Tecla has about her none of the pretensions associated with maternity: she is not proud, triumphant or blissful. She is engulfed in a situation nothing could prepare her for, overcome with emotion. She is not the Madonna of Lotti or Bellini, demure with the heavenly task bestowed upon her; Tecla is fragile and human, confused and scared, and full of all the hopes and dreams in the world.

---

[12] When Brenda and Brandon aren't doing their chores they're helping the homeless or saving the environment.

Ugo Rondinone's work seems to fly straight off the red hot catwalks of Milan. His soft-focus target paintings create a throbbing backdrop for his ventures as a 'model'. In Rondinone's fashion photos his head is cleverly transplanted onto the bodies of the beautiful and glamorous: Rondinone plays a *Super-model/waif/tramp*. Even his black and white photo-negative-ish landscape drawings are of the *Now…*

There is something about a Parisian whore which is a thousand times more enticing than a Malibu aerobics instructor. Portrayed by Shirley Maclaine[13], Marlene Dietrich[14] et al. the post of *la femme dévergondé* has been idolised by Maugham and Sartre, immortalised by Toulouse-Lautrec, Picasso. She is the working man's[15] temptress, her head held high in the trashy dignity of a woman of love. And in Love Rondinone is.

Adorning his red light district with neon beacons, Rondinone presents his large target paintings. Titled in sequence *(No.88 VIERTERJANUARNEUNZEHNHUNDERTSIEBENUNDNEUNZIG)*, he nostalgicises and fixates us with a specific memory, a dream. Venal supernovas: we are hypnotised into a portal of electric mysticism, TV sex, a whirlwind of consumer speciousity.

Formalistically following the tradition of Kenneth Noland, in content Rondinone's bull's eyes reference photography more than paint: these are the colours and textures of Maybelline®, this is the out of focus magnetism of film, the soft porn of advertising.

Within his world of swirling street lights and wanton passion, Rondinone becomes the object of *desire*. Cunningly manipulated photos place Rondinone's own visage on to the bodies of supermodels, resulting not in camp or parody, but in a deceiving amorphism; these fashion photos play on the hard-core.

> ***I Don't Live Here Anymore:*** Bleached hair crimped, makeup hard edged. Black mid-rif top by [Stephen Sprouse, $180][16]. The gaze over his anaemic shoulder is Attitude, Seduction, Violence, Street Smart (it's like Rap before rap was Gangsta). Rondinone is a Vamp, a Man-eater, he's Madonna c.1983.
>
> ***I Don't Live Here Anymore:*** Hair by [Boy Meets Girl], Lingerie from [Sax $145]. Rondinone is the baby doll, the gaunt stomached, rose nippled nymph. Torrid and pouty, he teases us by cropping the photo just short.
>
> ***I Don't Live Here Anymore:*** Cocaine-Rock-Star-Groupie-Glam-Girl, Rondinone vexes and begs. He's a She-Devil, a bad little girl. He wants you to come out and play. Silver top and gold boots by [Valentino: $625, $1249].

---

[13] <u>Irma La Douce</u> **(1963).**

[14] <u>The Blue Angel</u> **(1930).** <u>Morocco</u> **(1930).**

[15] The women Rondinone becomes are not of the 'classy' variety. This is not to say that they couldn't be the fantasy of minor royalty and the like, but seem to be more likely to adorn the arms of the 'common man's rock star'. Rondinone wouldn't look out of place in a Dire Straits video or in *Arena* as the latest girlfriend of a Gallagher Brother.

[16] [This is pure conjecture in my *Marks and Spencer* world.]

The overt sexual gestures of the models, once feminine and alluring, now take on a new form: it's not drag, it's not trans-sexual, it's *kinky*, deliciously perverse. In the safely inaccessible confines of the freeze-frame, he is the intangible object of desire. S/he's all the more lascivious.

Within the same series, *I Don't Live Here Anymore*, Rondinone has shifted the source of his fantasy from the lust for the ultramodern to the sultry romance of cinematic lore. Bathed in the red light of prostitution, these photos are much more reminiscent of the literary Euro-myths from the years around the wars. Bohemianism, cabaret, cigarettes and absinthe, existentialism and the musky smell of sweat.

> ***I Don't Live Here Anymore:*** Adorned in feathers and a beret, Rondinone looks shamelessly into the camera while he lazily smokes a fag and dangles a naked leg. A faceless conquest lounges in the background.
>
> ***Morocco (film, 1930):*** Marlene Dietrich vamps, feather boa teasing, her siren "What Am I Bid For My Apples". Squalid haunt: The handsome Legionnaire refuses the fruit she offers him: "I always pay for what I get."
>
> Giving her his entire weeks pay, she hands him an apple....and the key to her room.

Rondinone enamours us with nostalgia, with scenes idealised in Hollywood, representing Europe to the world. Within these seedy clichéd scenes, Rondinone is the pouting, distracted *femme fatale*: lurid, risqué and sexy as hell.

Tracing back this idea of European erotica, Rondinone also presents images of the Romantic landscape: *No.69*, *No.70*. As well as referencing the Enlightened institution of the Pleasure Garden, these large ink drawings bring to mind the original sin of Albrecht Dürer's *Adam and Eve*. Caught in the negative light of the flash-bulb, these timeless pictures of romance become as fleeting and disposable as the latest trends in fashion.

Demand's large format photos are eerily empty. Perfect, flat lit, suburban coloured interiors lay out for us seamless presentations of life - almost computer-generated images inspired by an Ikea catalogue, these scenes offer little to the viewer other than chilling exactness. If these rooms look a little bit set up, that's because they are...

> **_Corridor:_** Three cheerless yellow doors: one will lead to Jeffrey Dahmer's[17] apartment[18]. Dahmer's crimes so heinous; his apartment so regular: This domestic view of the hallway almost normalises him, making the contemplation of the actual space nearly impossible. Somehow, even worse than being the next unsuspecting tenant to rent the Dahmer flat would be the person with the apartment next to it.[19]

The harmless solitude of the cemetery is always a real source of terror in the active imagination/In America, Charles Manson is interviewed on television as entertainment. Perhaps it is this confused conception of real horror that is a driving force in the work of Thomas Demand. After all, Demand believes in ghost stories more than we do.

It is the premise in horror movies that evil will cling to the place of its origin, waiting with festering enmity to possess its next inhabitants. The fiends of the screen become heroes of our fantasy: their haunts vestiges of their immortality. Malevolence is always fuelled by the potential for a sequel.[20]

> **_Archive:_** A vault full of Nazi-glorifying film footage by Leni Riefenstahl: one canister is missing...

Each of Demand's life sized sets are entirely constructed from paper. Modelled with excruciating detail from archive photos, Demand chooses to reconstruct 'crime scenes' with forensic accuracy: each treated with the same documentary sense of suspicion, suspension and qualm. Sharing the desolation of Edward Hopper and not-quite-right eeriness of Cindy Sherman's film stills, Demand's 'virtual realities' are perhaps most disturbing because they do something that

---

[17] Convicted Pedophile, Kidnapper, Rapist, Pornographer, Murderer, Necrophile and Cannibal, Jeffery Dahmer found Jesus in prison and turned to a quite, peaceful life of incarcerated repentance. He was killed by another prisoner with a mop while on cleaning duty.

[18] Oxford Apartments, #213, 924 North 25th Street, Milwaukee, Wisconsin. Although cautioned several times by police for complaints from neighbours and victims, investigation was never furthered as Dahmer's apartment was always extraordinarily neat and tidy (although smelled really bad). During a casual visit from the police investigating another complaint, suspicion was finally aroused by the discovery of a human head in his refrigerator. All the gruesome details are at
http://www.crimellbrary.com/dahmer/dahmermain.htm

[19] If this prospect doesn't scare you, watch **The Candyman.**

[20] Horror movies aren't just an American phenomenon: Wagner, Werner Hammer House, Maximo all cashed in on the chiller craze. Differences being the US preference for the (non-historically founded) Psychopath or Zombie vs. the Euro-thriller's contentment to use the tried and true Vampire, Werewolf and Mad-Scientist themes.

virtual reality never intended: they re-create the real.[21] These are photos of contemporary legends, the real-life media-friendly horror stories of popular gossip.

> ***Zimmer:*** Weirder-than-Science-fiction Sect founder L.Ron Hubbard has a Rasputin-like hold over his followers.[22] As compelling a secret as an Alchemist's lab, as holy a sanctum as the Vatican's vaults, Demand's reconstruction of the hotel room where Dianetics was penned somehow re-confirms our worse suspicions[23].

Each scene more blank than the next: Demand's romance lies in the unsaid.[24]

---

[21] Computer-Jah Bill Gates proclaims a monetary hierarchical value in and consequently the concrete existence of visual perfection. Gates owned Corbis Corporation currently owns over 23 million images of varying 'perfectness' (ranging from celebrity pics, news items to fine art). Digitally 'watermarked': a fee must be paid for their use…. Howard Hughes-ishly eccentric, Gates is one of the most despised men in the world. A quick peruse of YAHOO! Brings up 92 Bill Gates Web sites, some titles of which are: ***Decapitate Bill Gates***, ***Bill Gates is the Devil***, ***I Hate Bill Gates*** and ***The Society for the Prevention of Bill Gates Gets Everything***. Gates is so dark, Demand has even made a photograph of his space. (But it's not in this book, so you'll have to look elsewhere!)You can email Bill at **billg@microsoft.com** or **billg40@tiac.net**

[22] Science-fiction author turned cult-leader, Hubbard's ***Dianetics: The Modern Science of Mental Health*** (1950) solves the "riddles of the human mind". Church of Scientology members include John Travolta, Kirstie Alley and Tom Cruise. For an endlessly long and dubious account of Hubbard's achievements go to **http://www.authorservicesinc.com/ata_home.htm**.

[23] Shrouded in secrecy, there are many vicious rumours about the sect: "Scientology is quite likely the most ruthless, the most classically terroristic, the most litigious and the most lucrative cult the country has ever seen." **http://come.to/irc.scientology**

[24] Shhhhh! (a secret): ***Büro*** is the remnants of the Stasi (Secret Police) HQ after it was raided by angry East German mobs searching for their personal files during the iron curtain collapse in 1989. Today everyone has the right to see their own file and copies can be ordered from the government. ***Zeichensaal*** represents the office of Robert Vorhoelzer, architectural visionary of post-war Germany. Most of München (Demand's hometown) was destroyed in the war, this new Modern style of building began replacing, *erasing*…. ***Spüle***: Dirty dishes have never been so scary…***Caution: Demand himself may dispute any of the explanations given here. Like in the X-files, the Truth of Demand's photos may never be known...***

The paintings of Juan Uslé are an embodiment of everything. Intense colours gesticulate in an almost systematic language of their own. Energy and plethora: streaks of speed, fissures of light, within the action you might see something that you almost recognise…

Uslé's paintings are labyrinths, computer circuitry melded with biomorphic form. Their beguiling colours, seamless textures draw us in; we are already captivated before we realise we are in the realm of the ominous. Hand-crafted in form, Uslé offers up a home-brew science fiction: the basement laboratory of the mad scientist, the underworld of Gotham City, the evident construction of a movie spaceship. As urban landscapes, these paintings are [futuristic?] contemporary… *Modern.*

> **_Rizoma's:_** These chemical colours oddly dark, painting out a cityscape of wonder and corruption. Keyboard buttons, computer chips, high-rise windows, electric cords, circuit boards, plumbing pipes, catacombs, pre-fab units, bio-waste, veins. Cobalt and Cadmium: The rhythm is moving, it's blood is racing, its… Alive. This looks like a game, it is a trap.

As non-mediated, regurgitated response to information bombardment, Juan Uslé taps into a collective fear of an *Atomic* generation: the hysteria of the mechanised era. Titles such as <u>Welcome to the Eye</u>, <u>Rizoma's</u> and <u>Yonkers Imperator</u> smack of the gothic teenage romance and haunting moralising predictions of Philip K. Dick[25] and Harlan Ellison[27]. These are visions of the future where machine masters man, humans are rendered obsolete and super-computers replace God. Abstracted to the overwhelmed mind of the mortal, Uslé races to catch it all.

Beguiled, he adapts, emulates and absorbs all he comes in contact with. <u>Yonker's Imperator</u> and <u>Mal de Sol</u> throw objects into space: non-gravitational, floating, this surrealism draws from Gaunt, from Tanguy. Jumping ahead to the 60's, <u>Sone que Revelabas</u> makes disorder of Frank Stella. <u>Lineas de Madras</u> and <u>Welcome to the Eye</u> offer an MTV blend of Adolph Gottlieb and Fiona Rae.

Uslé is a Romantic painter, painting the mythology of the contemporary West. In picturing a future which supersedes itself, Uslé plays out the roles of *Artiste* and Alchemist, the bequestor and inventor, his is a view of the pulse of the modern, a starting point for fantasy.

---

[25] Mega-famous sci-fi author. Most noted for **_Do Androids Dream of Electric Sheep?_** on which **Blade Runner** was based.

[26] Perhaps the scariest Sci-fi writer ever. Way worse than Stephen King and Clive Barker combined. To experience nauseating mechanised terror, beyond even Usle's scope, read: **"I Have No Mouth And I Must Scream"**, <u>*Machines That Think*</u>. **Ed. Isaac Asimov et.al. Harmondsworth, Middlesex: Penguin, 1983.**

Greedily, knowingly, we cling to the fantasy. Männikkö and Djikstra, Rondinone and Demand, Uslé: their seduction a success. Awareness of what lies beneath the myths is blissfully forsaken, their fictions deliciously devoured. Belief is suspended, *la liaison commencera...*

Each of these artists weaves an enticing web of deceit, a captivating call to entanglement. Toying with illusion/perception, these artists use (and deny) pre-existing mythologies to devise sagas of their own. They re-create with exacting precision that insouciant sophistication of legendary European romance: But *new*, in a *worldly* way. They know what we long for, they feed our desire: to feel pastoral and carefree, young and innocent, sexy and glamorous, and even a little bit scared. We yearn to feel enamoured, we long to fall in Love.

Enchanters entranced: It seems these Europeans are seduced themselves a little bit too... After all Europe is the land of Romance.

The love sick mistress gazes through the window. Her married lover lights her cigarette. The impossibility of their love: moral duty is thrown to the wind in the face of their dream. With fatalistic determination, she decides:

"Don't let's ask for the moon, we have the stars."[27]

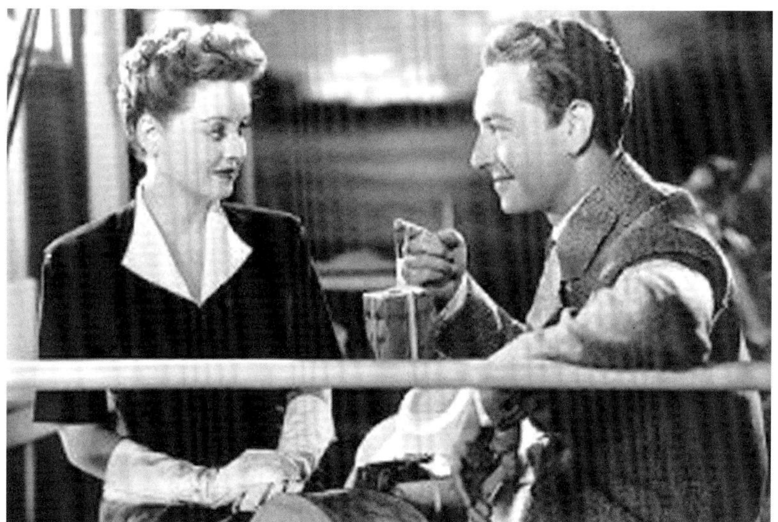

---

[27] Famous last scene from the most romantic movie ever! You know the one...

Büro (Office) 1996 183.5 x 240 cm

Zeichensaal (Drafting Room) 1996 183.5 x 285 cm

Archiv (Archive) 1995 183.5 x 233 cm

Zimmer 1996 172 x 232 cm

Flur (Corridor) 1996 183.5 x 270 cm

colour print diasec perspex

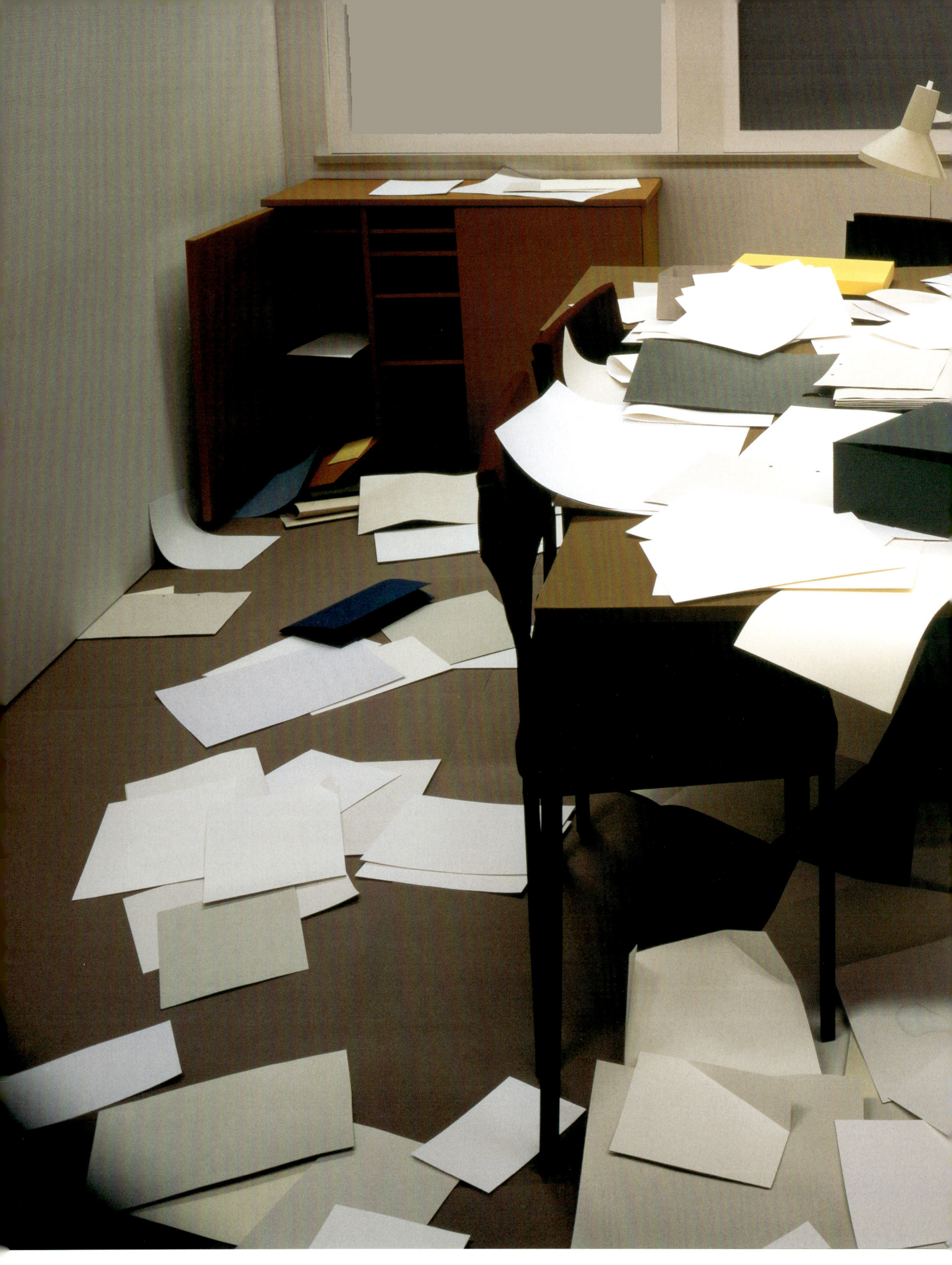

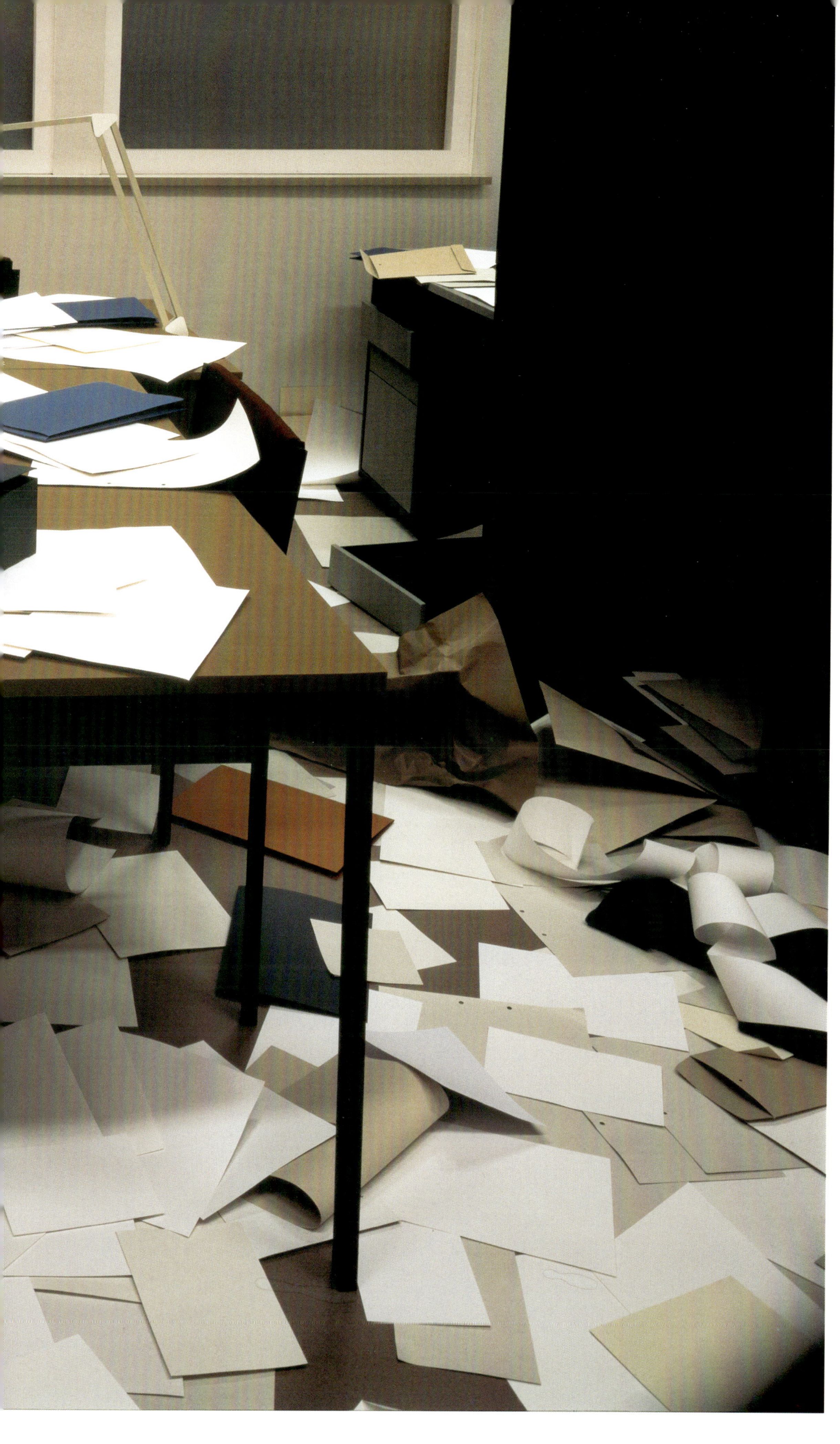

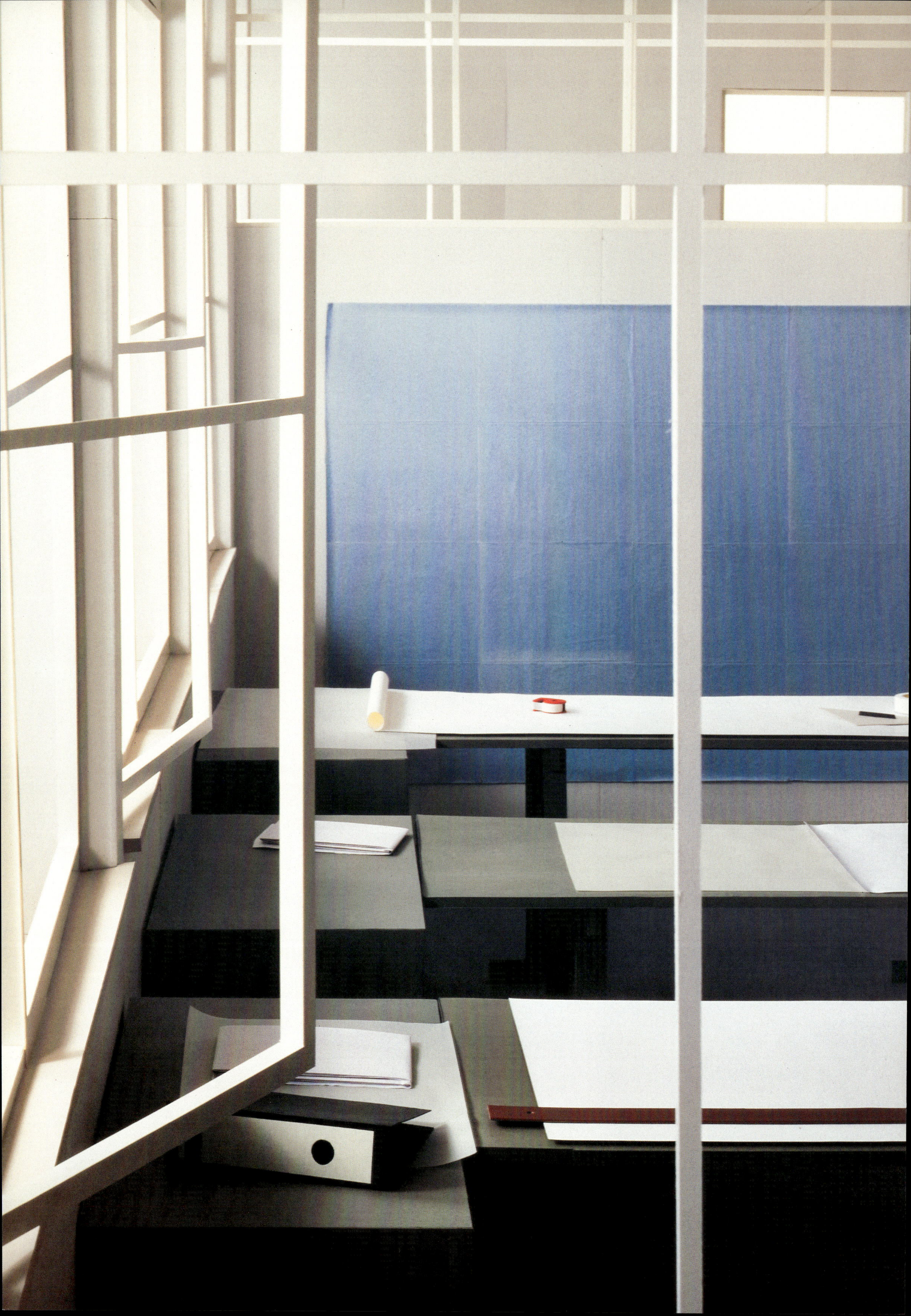

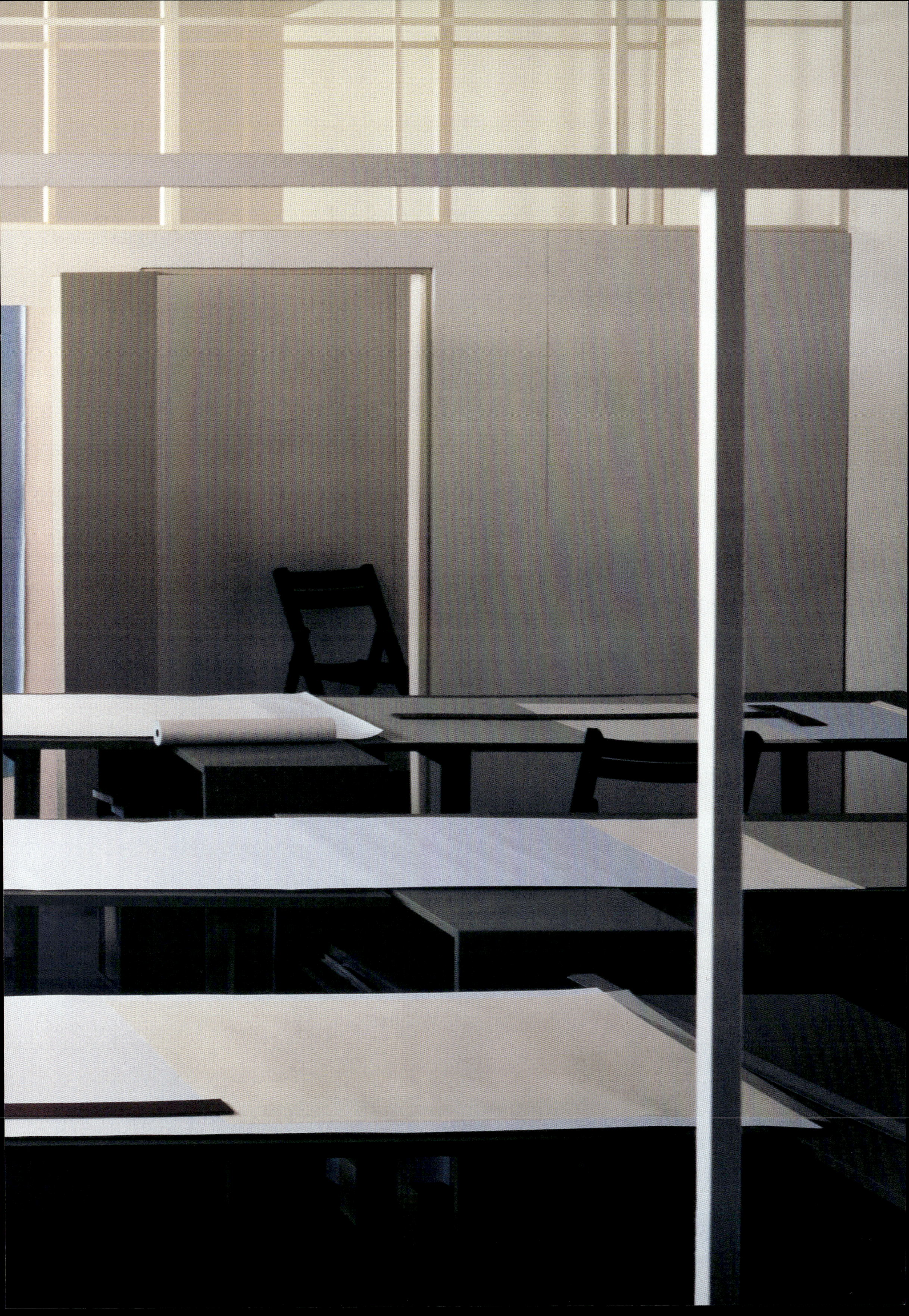

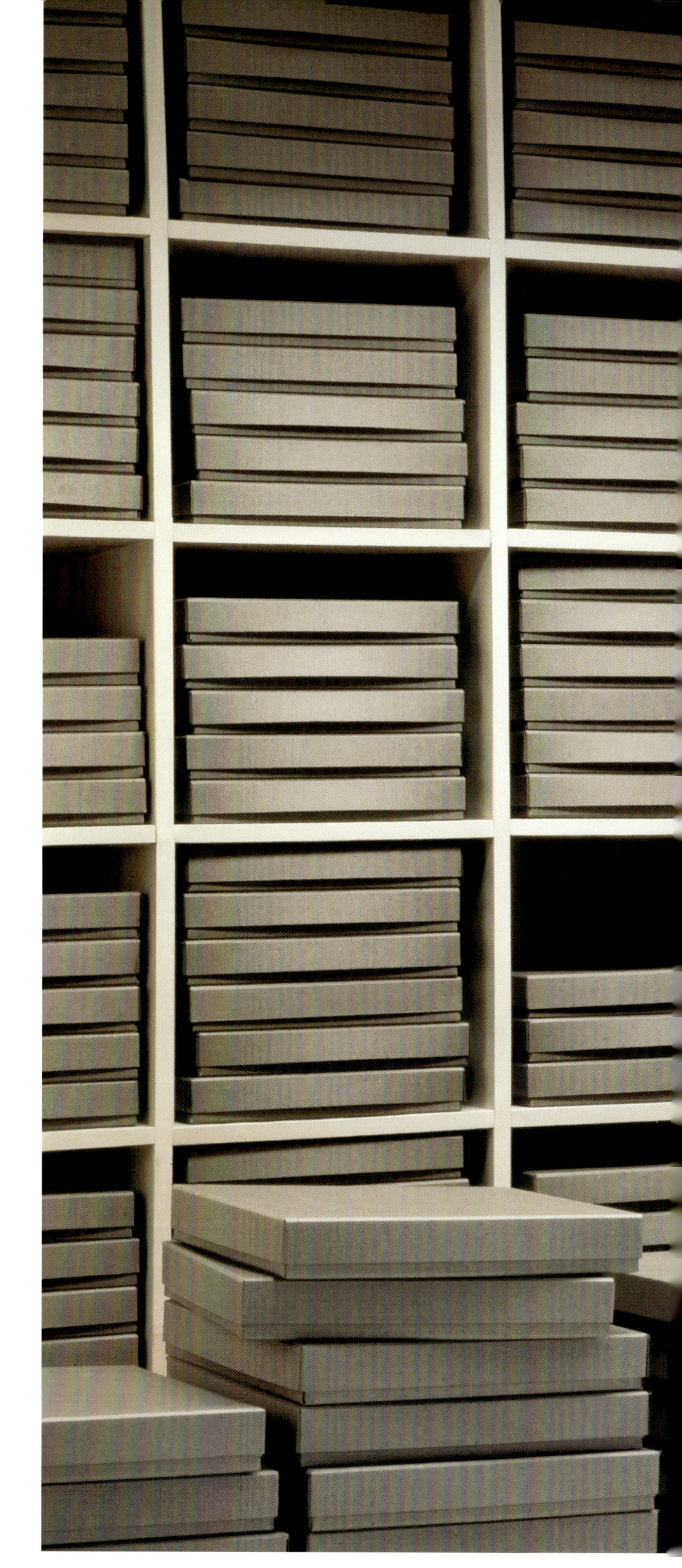

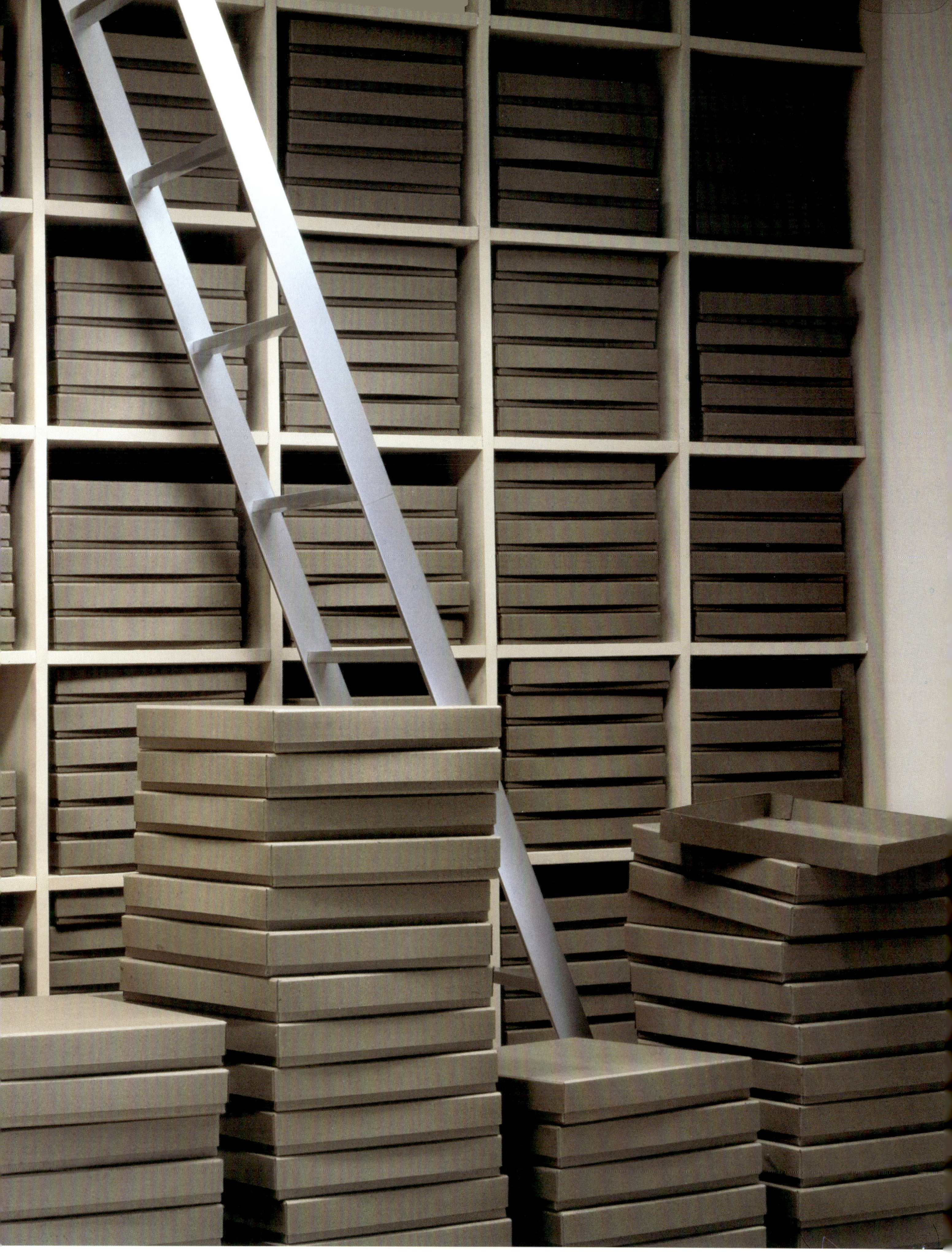

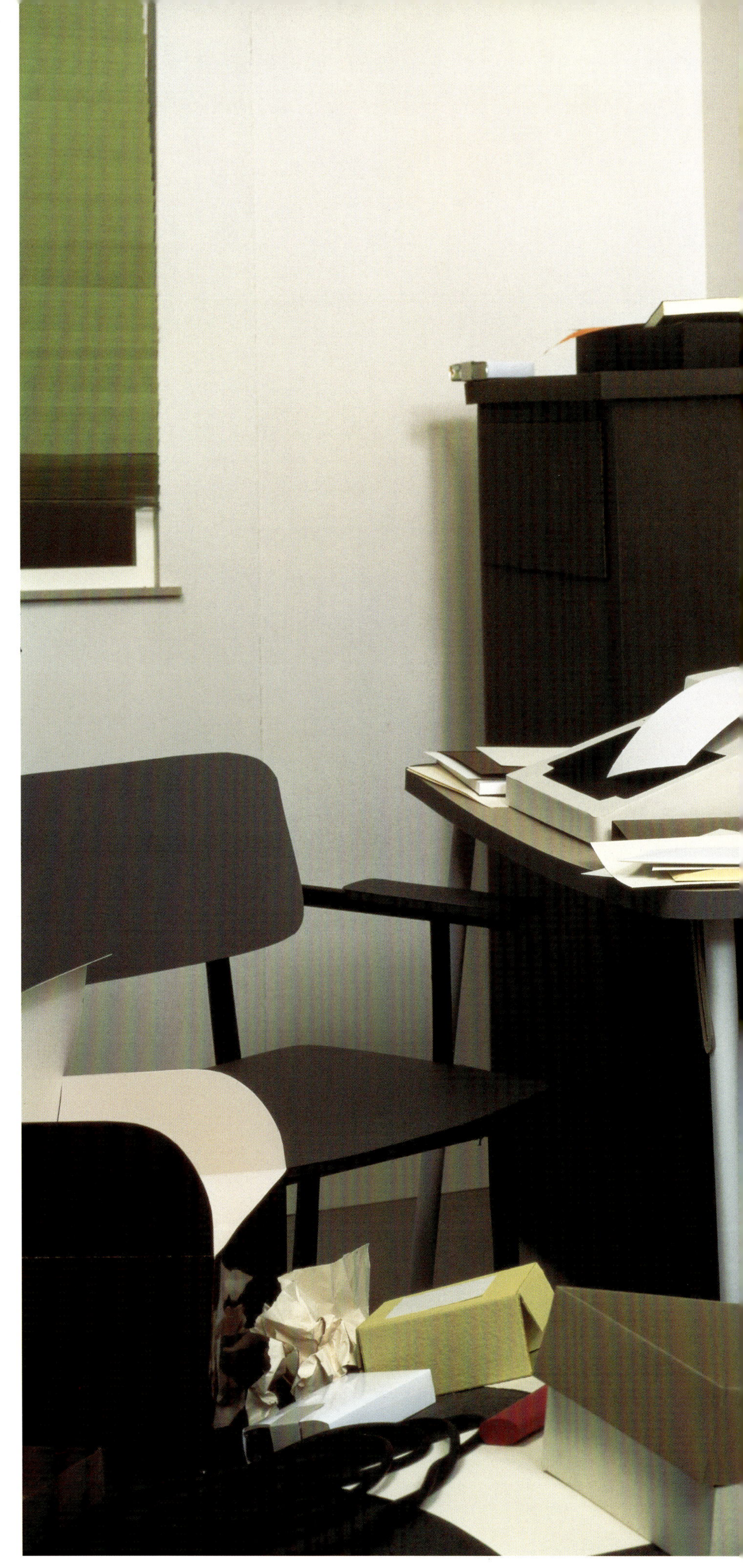

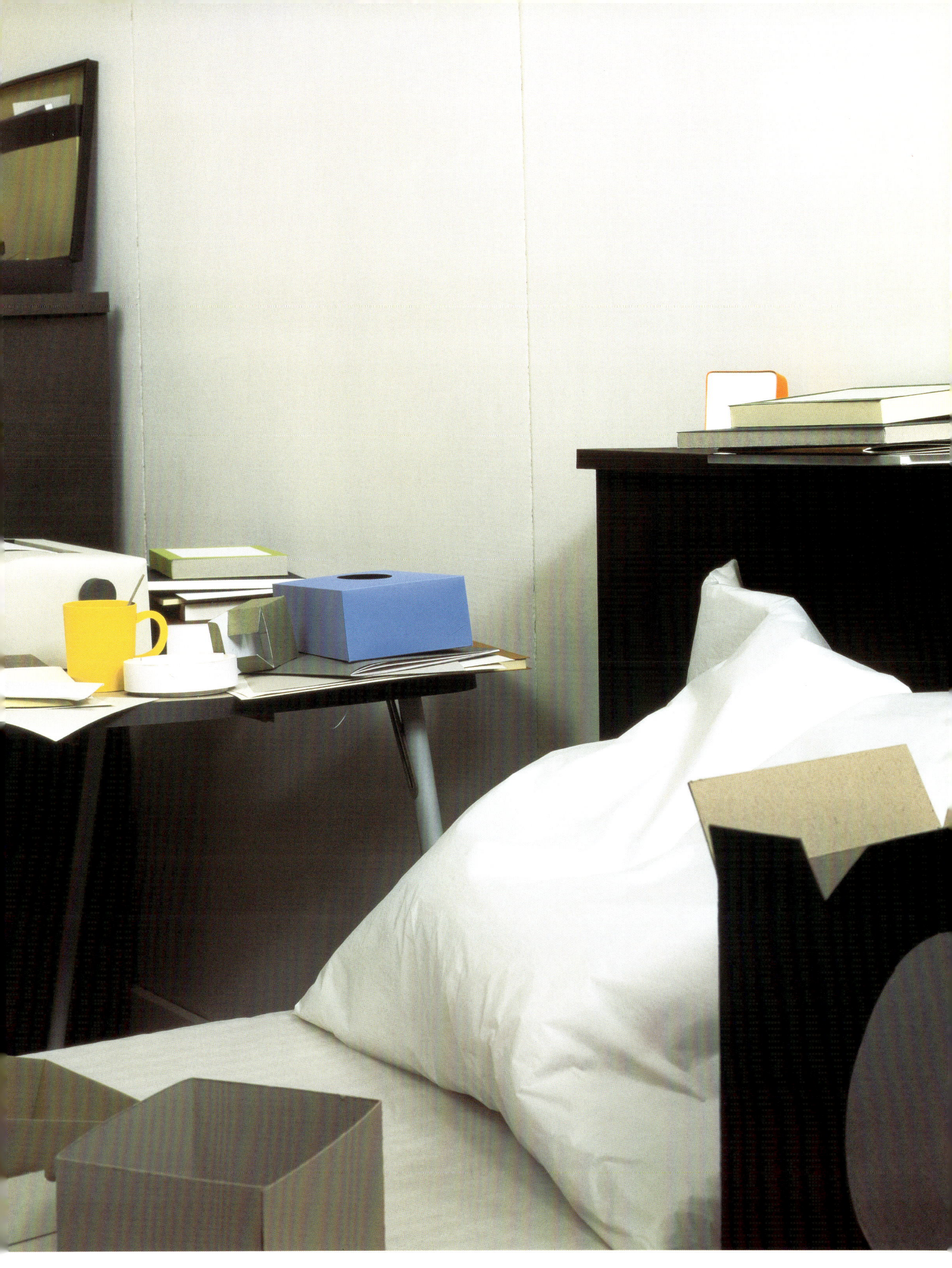

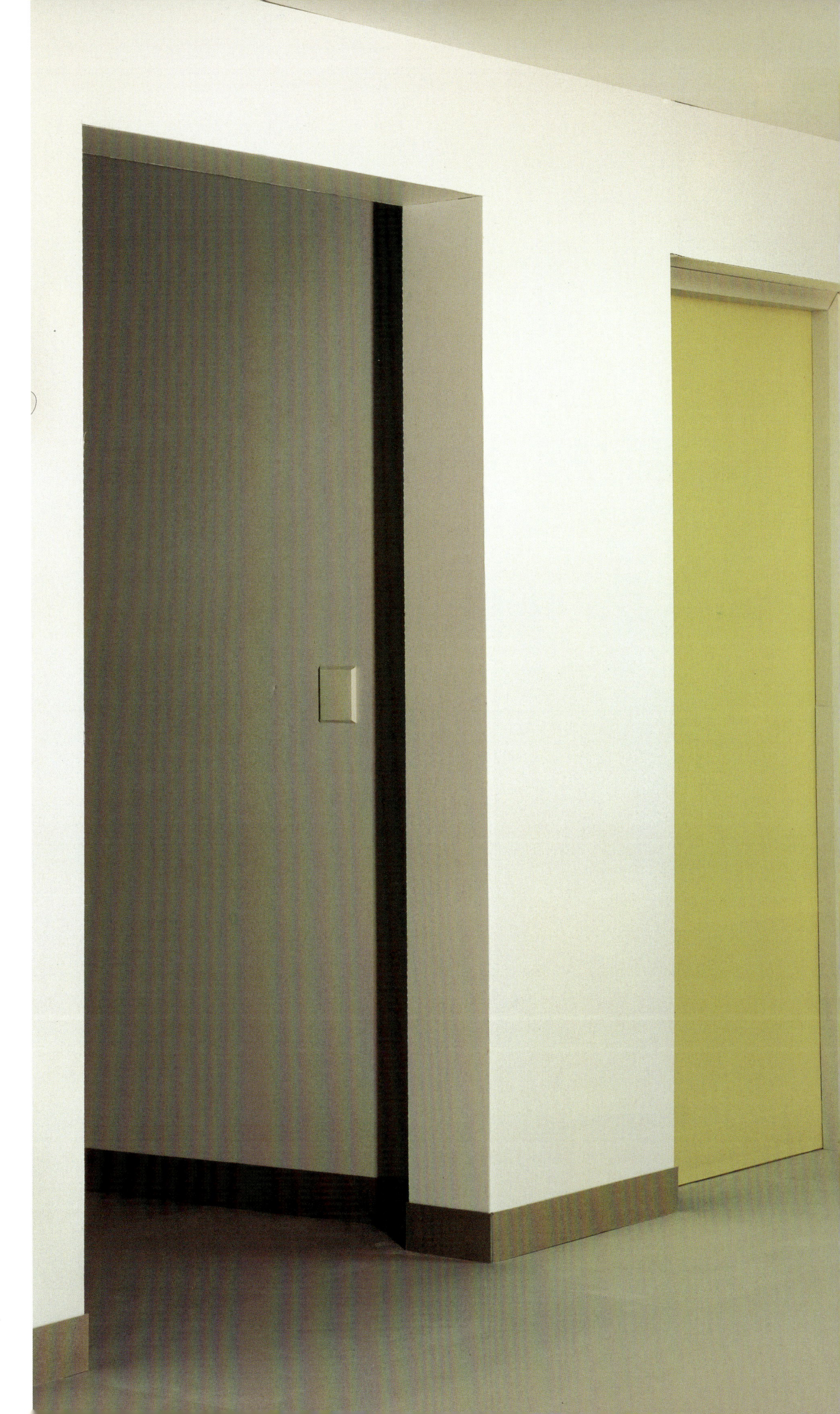

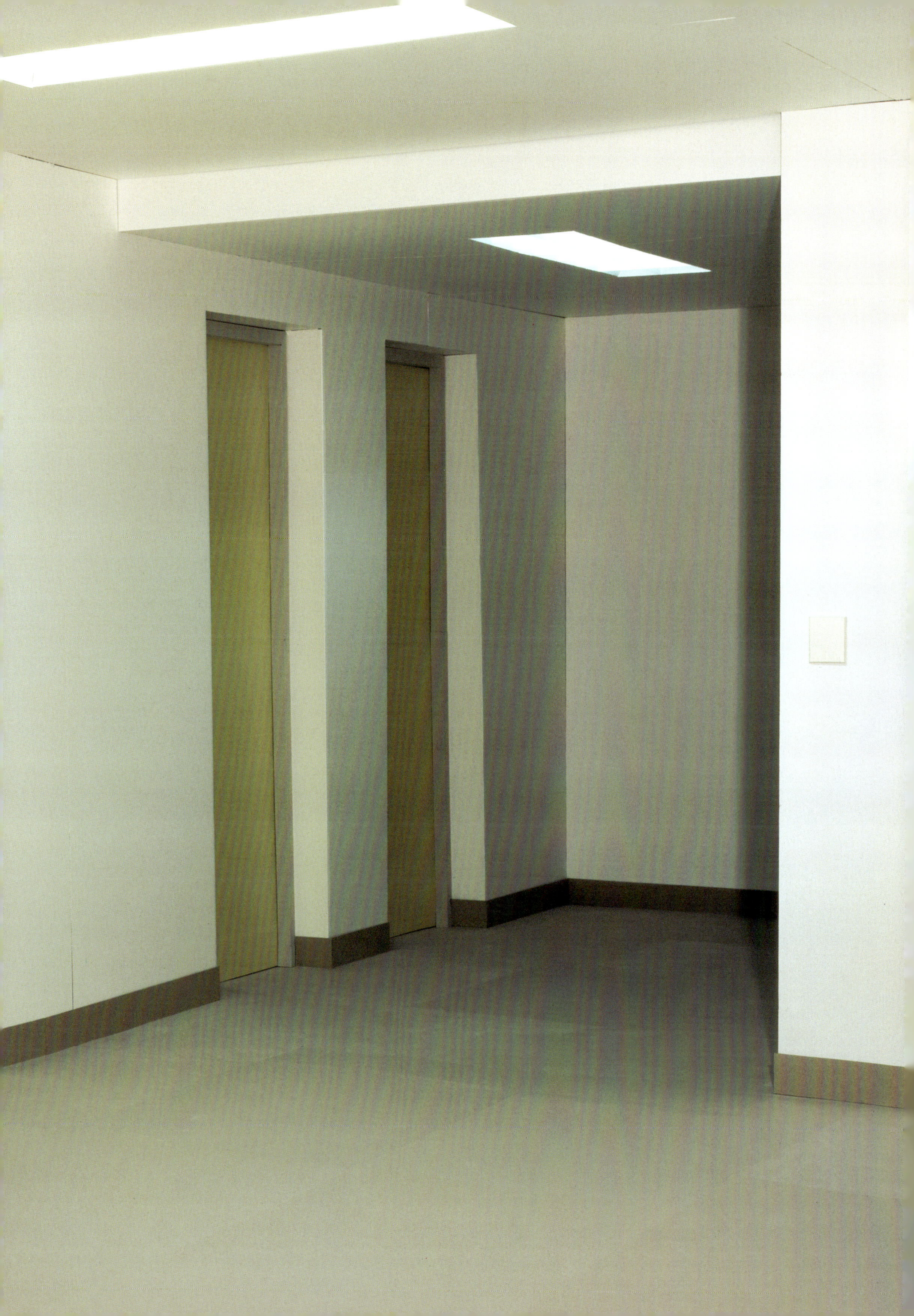

rineke **dijkstra**

Kolobrzeg, Poland, July 26, 1992

Coney Island, N. Y., USA, June 20, 1993

De Panne, Belgium, August 7, 1992

Odessa, Ukraine, August 4, 1993

Dubrovnik, Croatia, July 13, 1996

Hilton Head Island, S. C., USA, June 24, 1992
190 x 156 cm

Saskia Harderwijk, Netherlands, March 16, 1994

Tecla, Amsterdam, Netherlands, May 16, 1994

Julie, Den Haag, Netherlands, February 29, 1994
154 x 130 cm
colour print

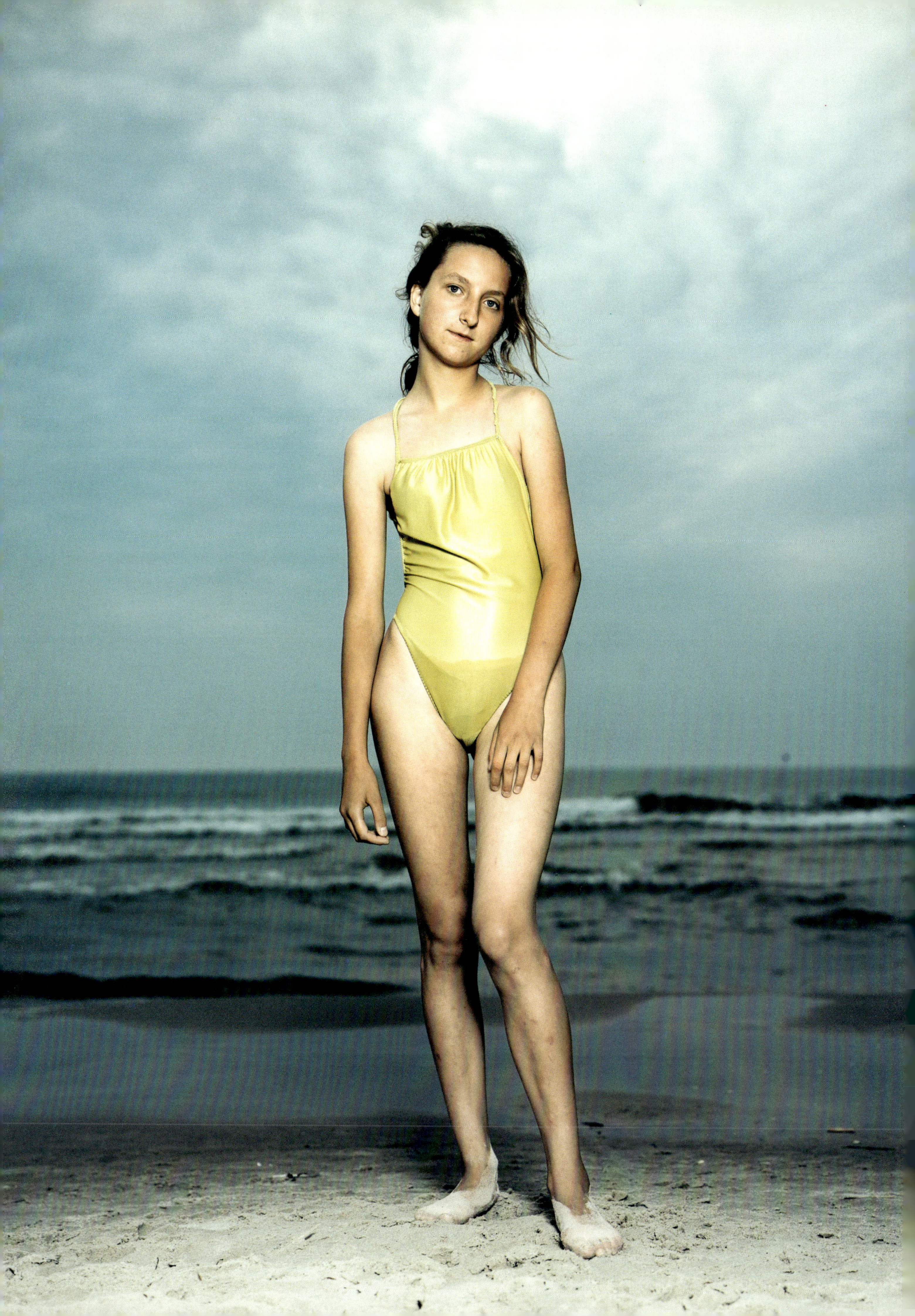

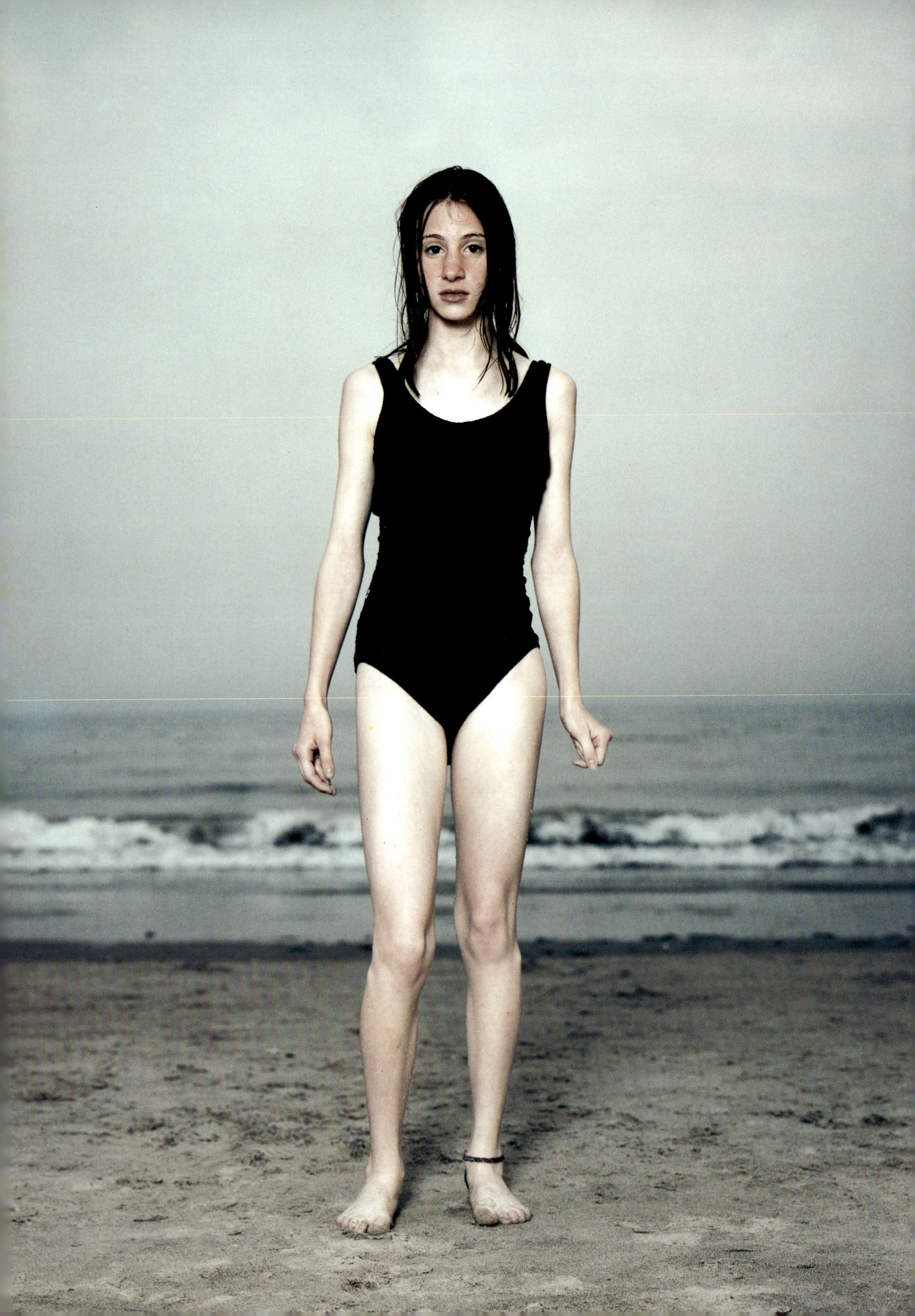

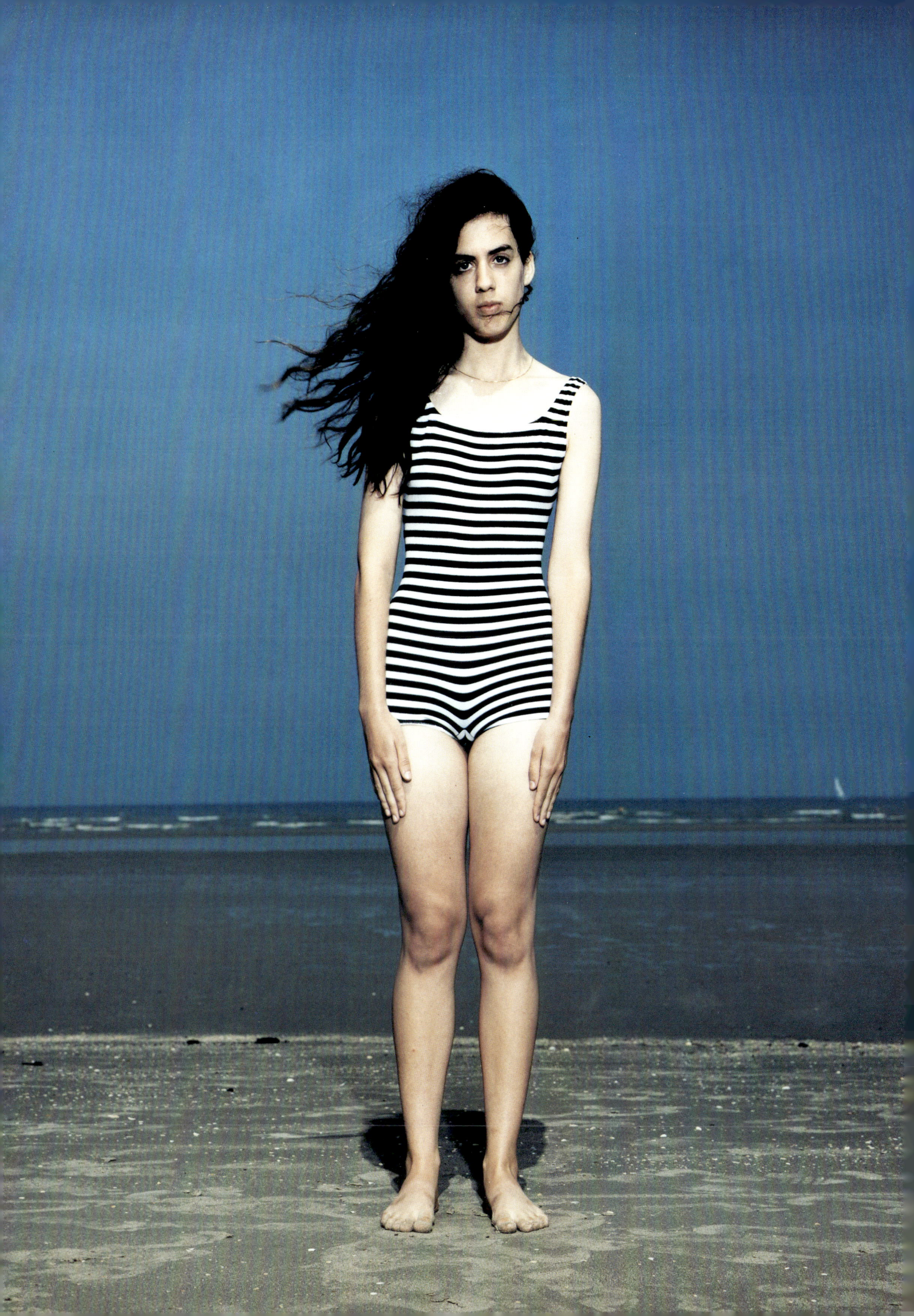

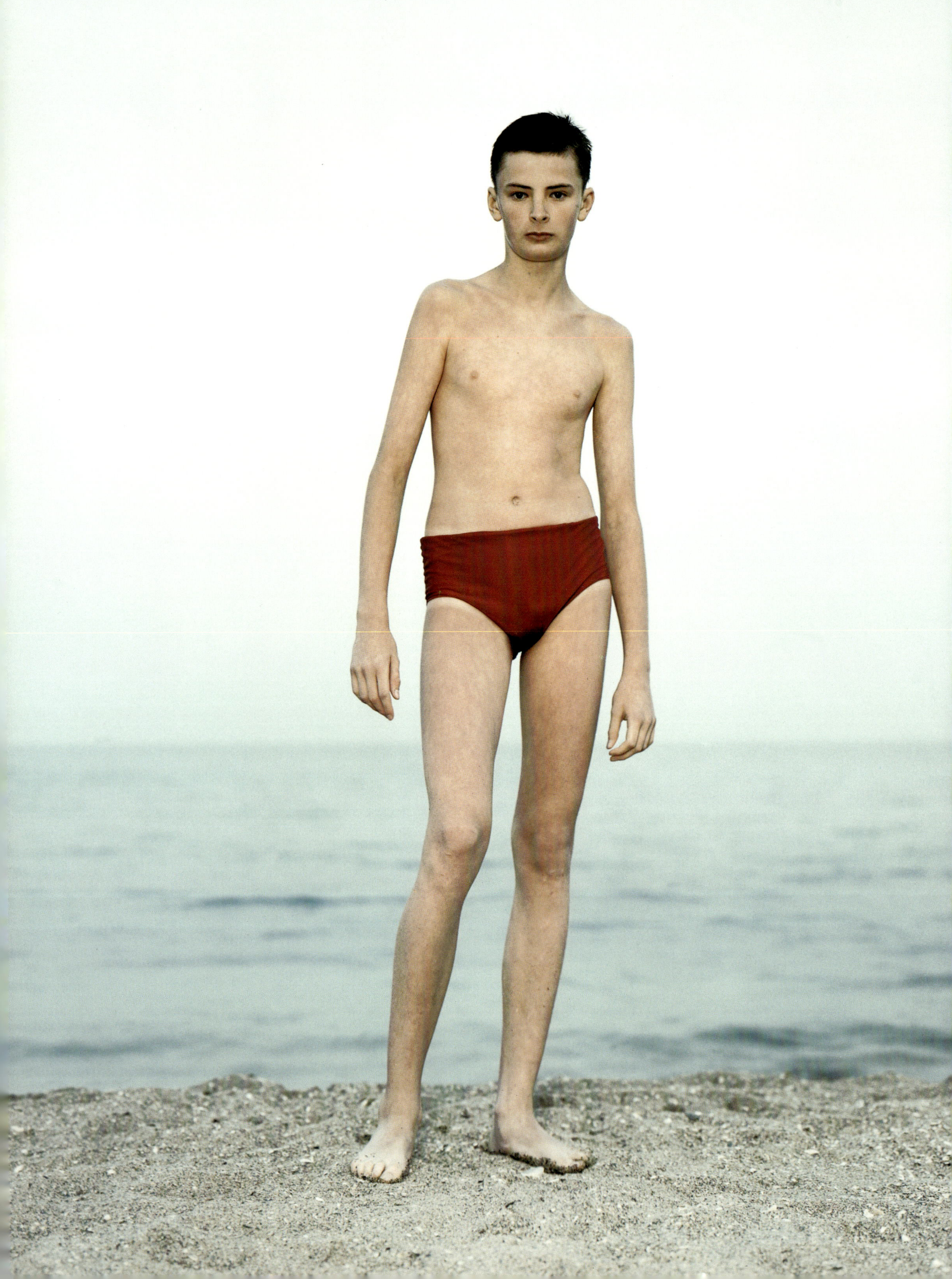

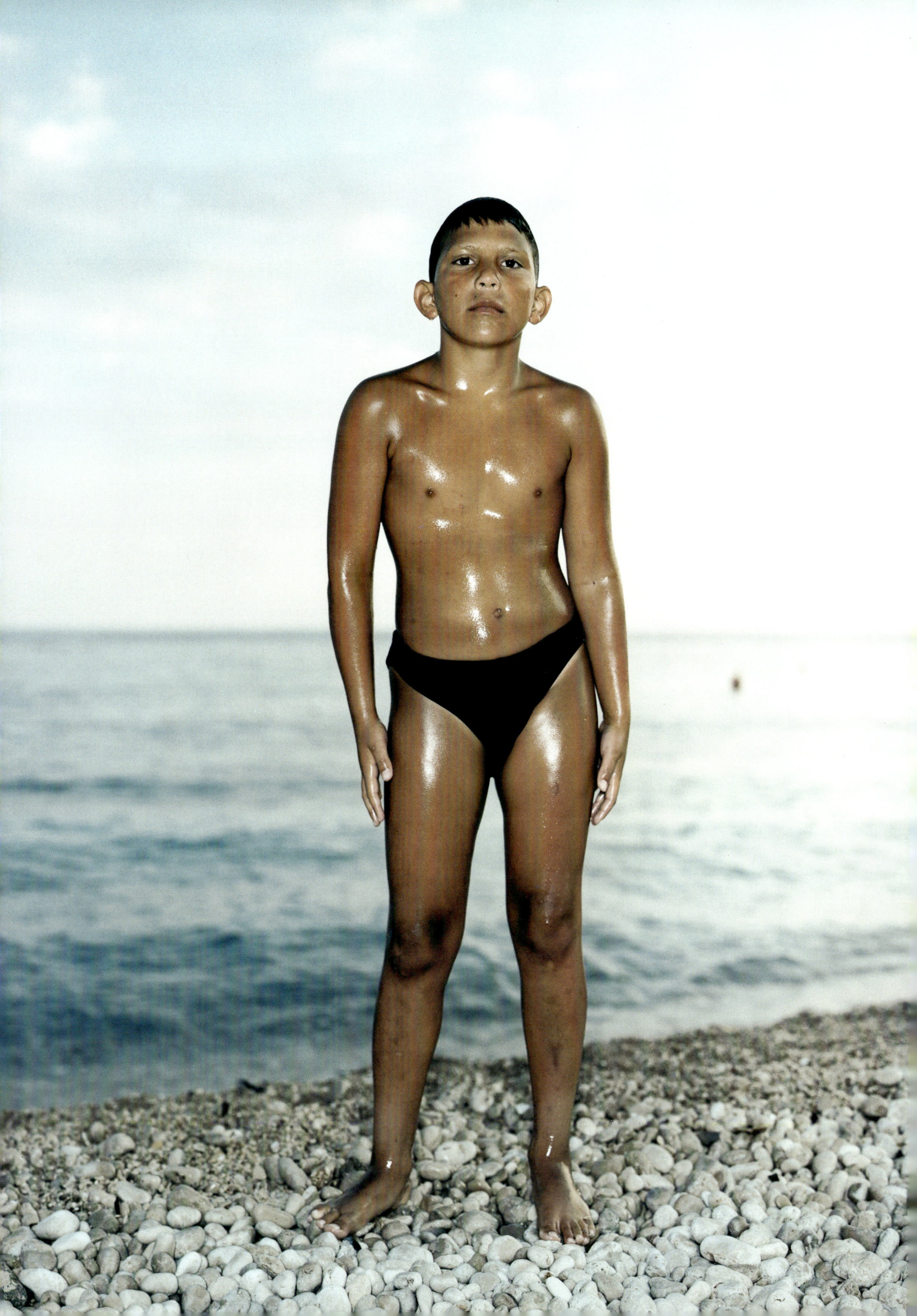

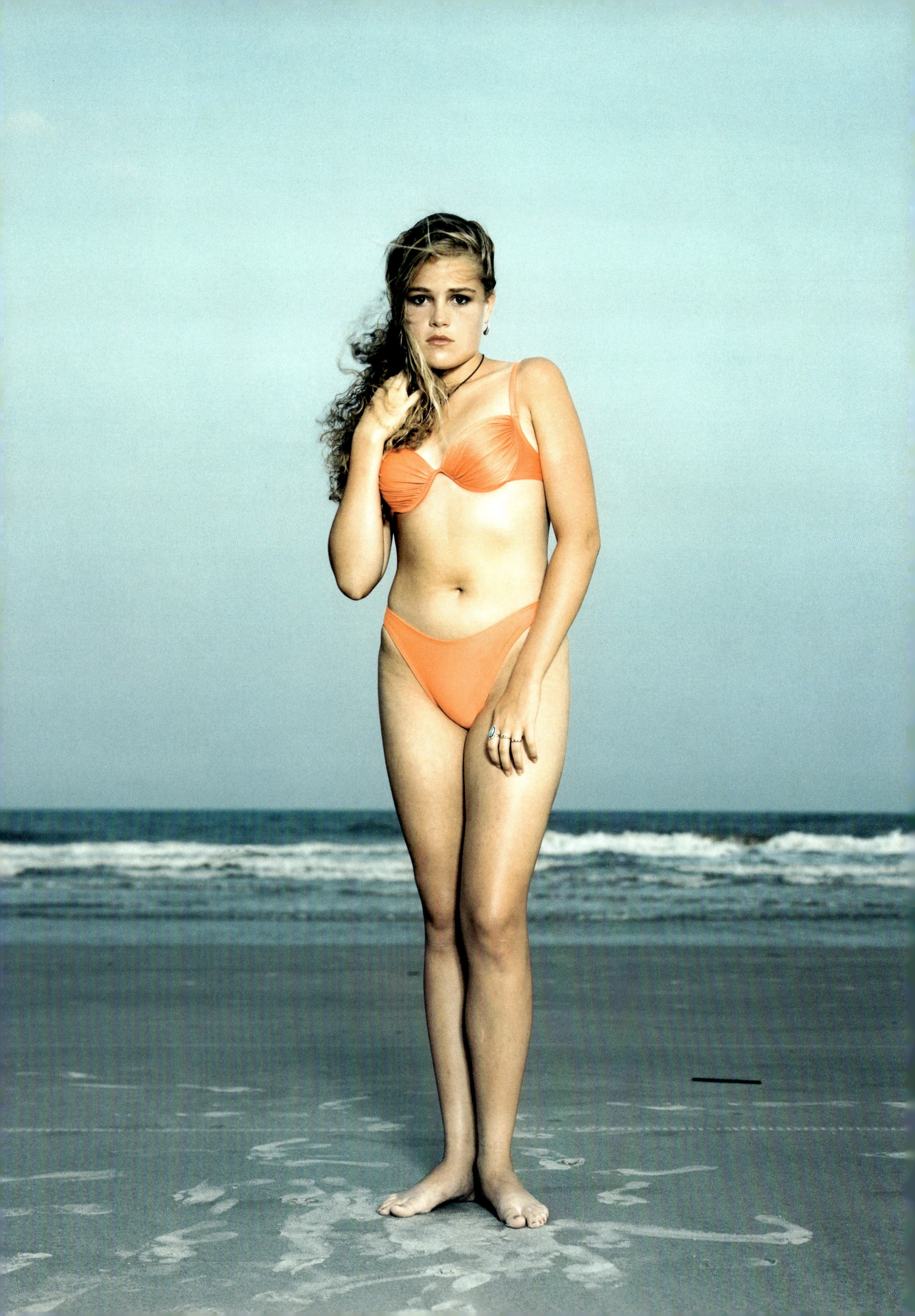

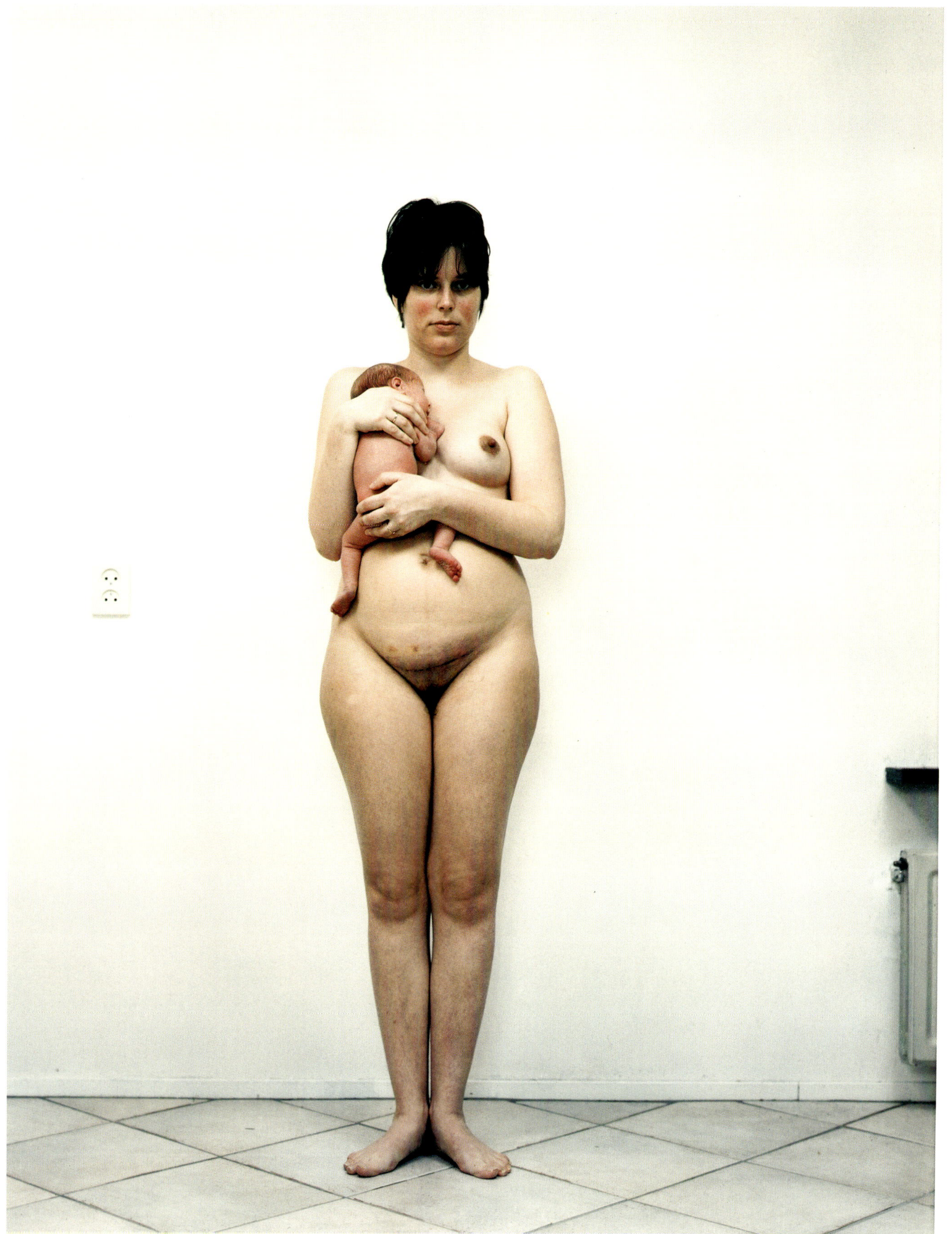

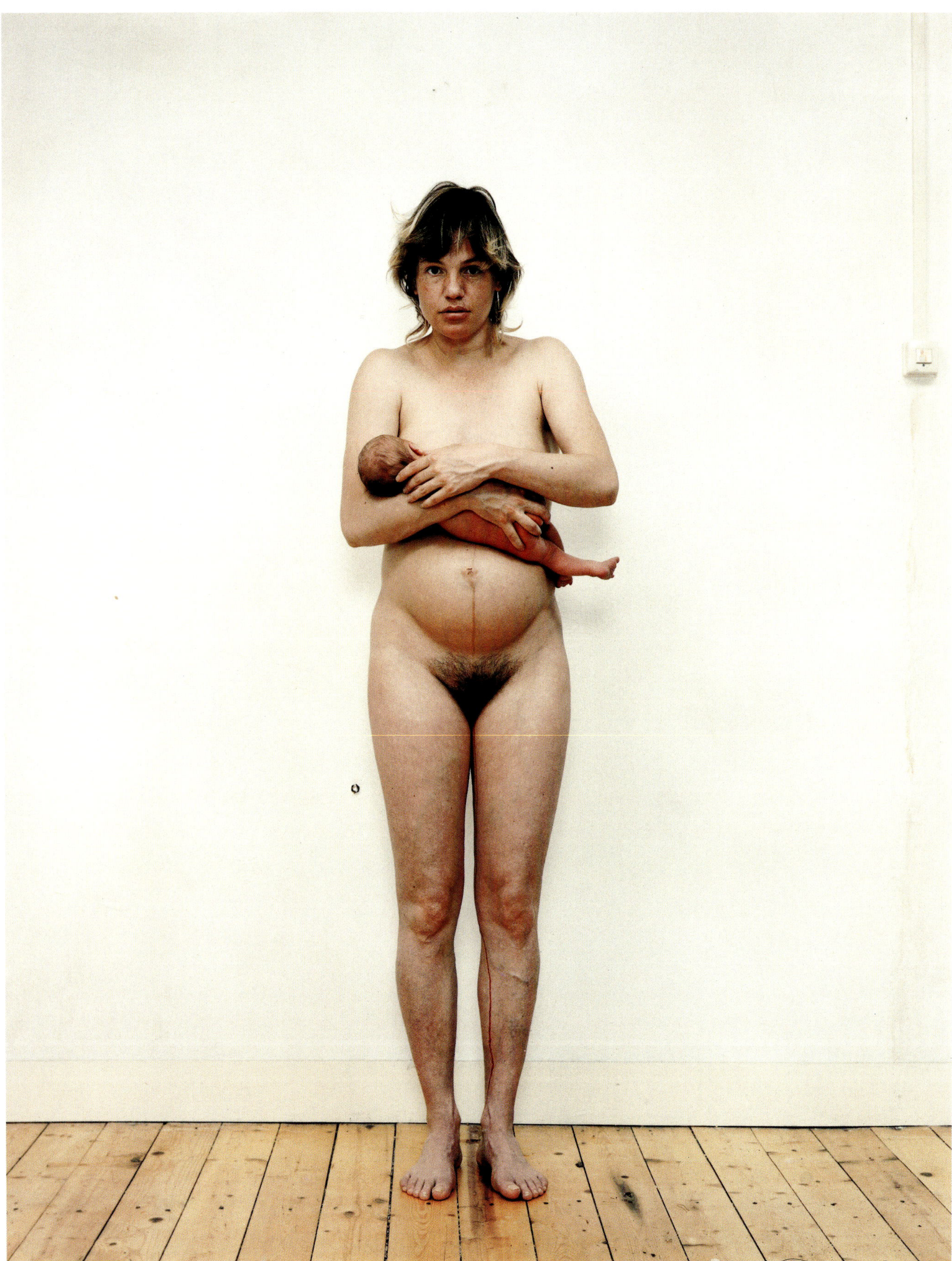

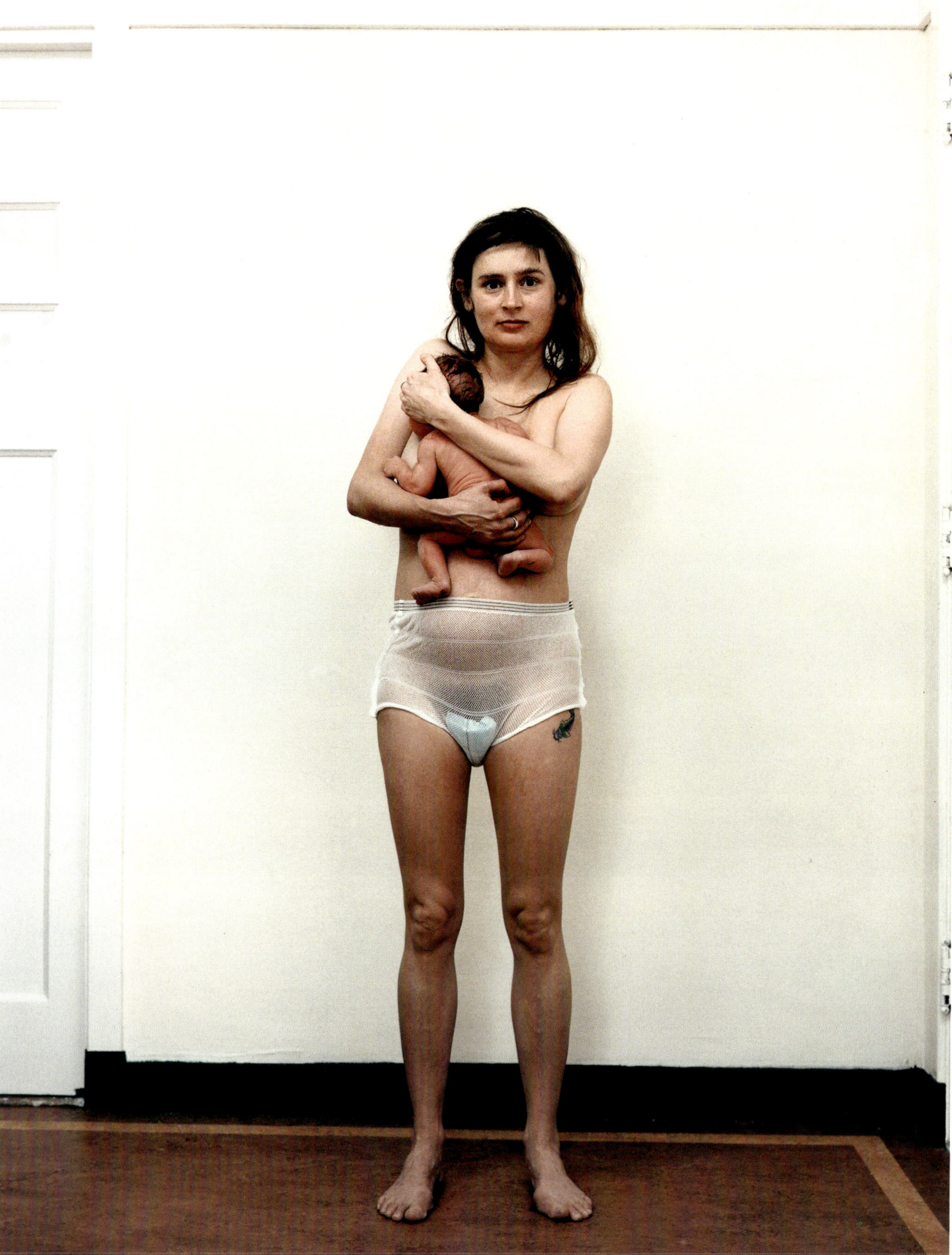

esko **männikkö**

Kuivaniemi 1993   62 x 71 cm

Ii 1995   50 x 60 cm

Kuivaniemi 1991   54 x 64 cm

Savukoski 1994   54 x 63 cm

Kuivaniemi 1993   64 x 54 cm

Savukoski 1995   55 x 66 cm

Savukoski 1994   53 x 63 cm

Utajärvi 1991   51 x 62 cm

Alex, Batesville 1997   70 x 150 cm

Romeo and his son, Carrizo Springs 1996   70 x 85 cm

Cowboy 1996   76 x 94 cm

Frank and Christina, San Antonio 1996   74 x 98 cm

framed photograph

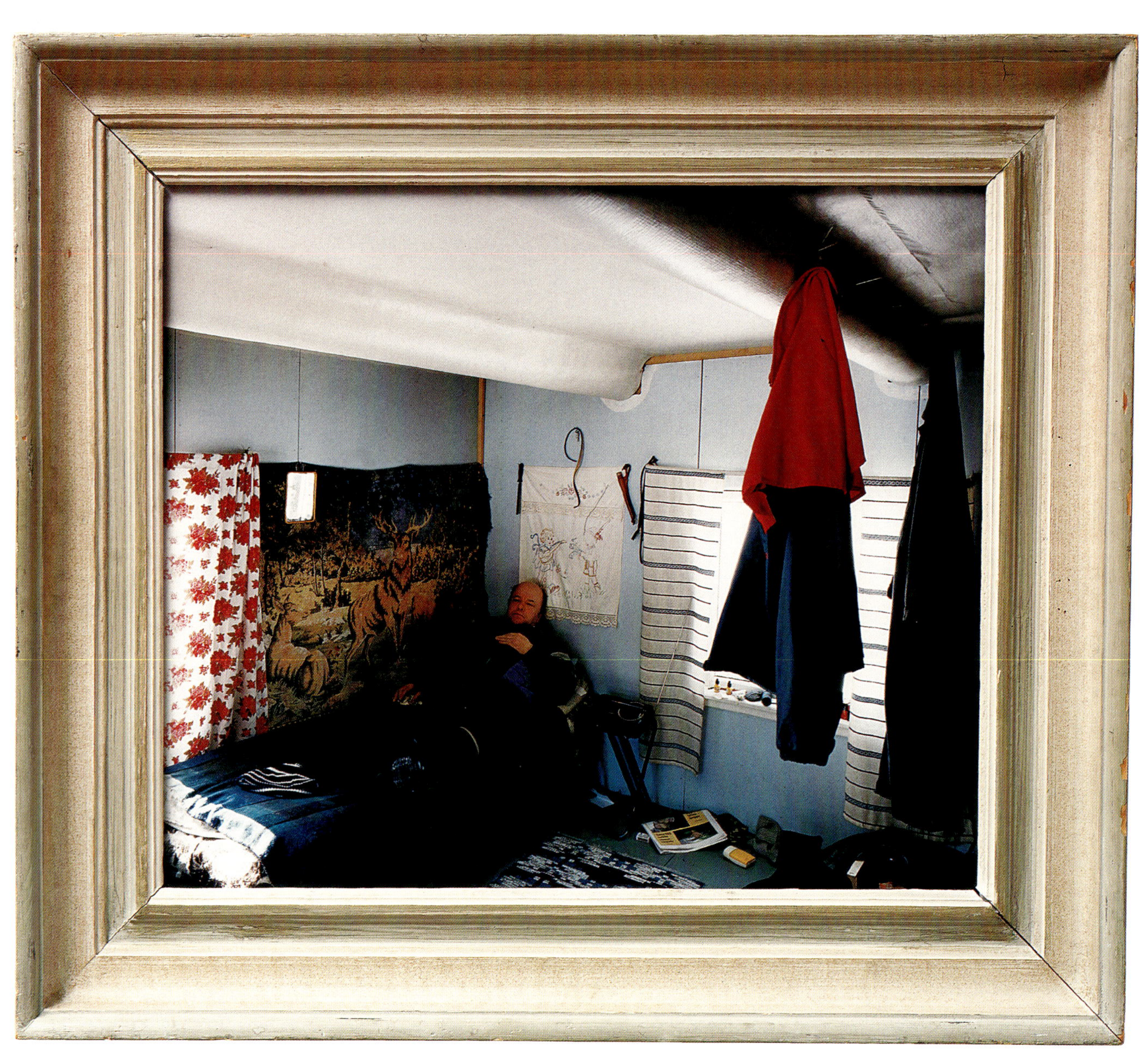

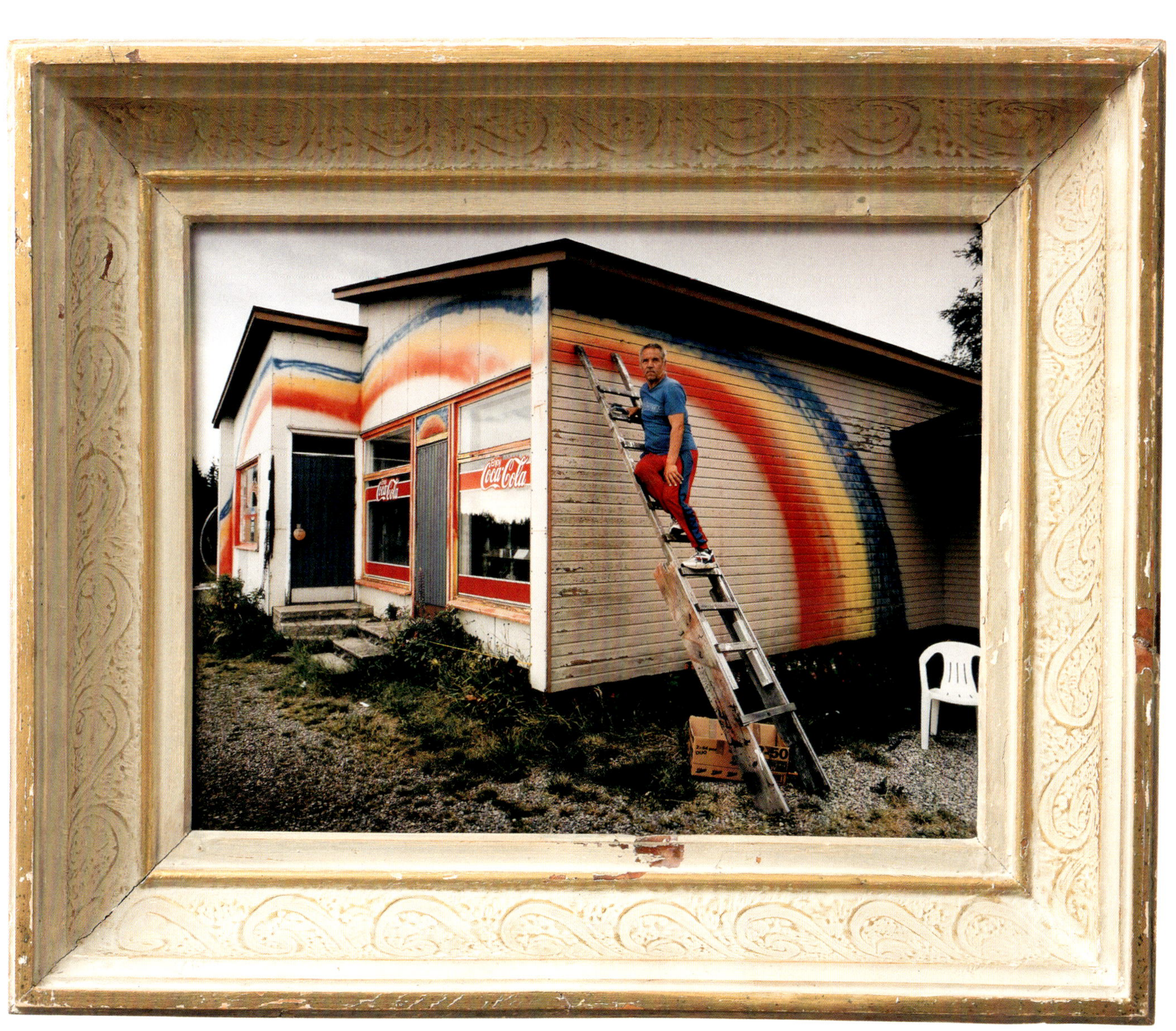

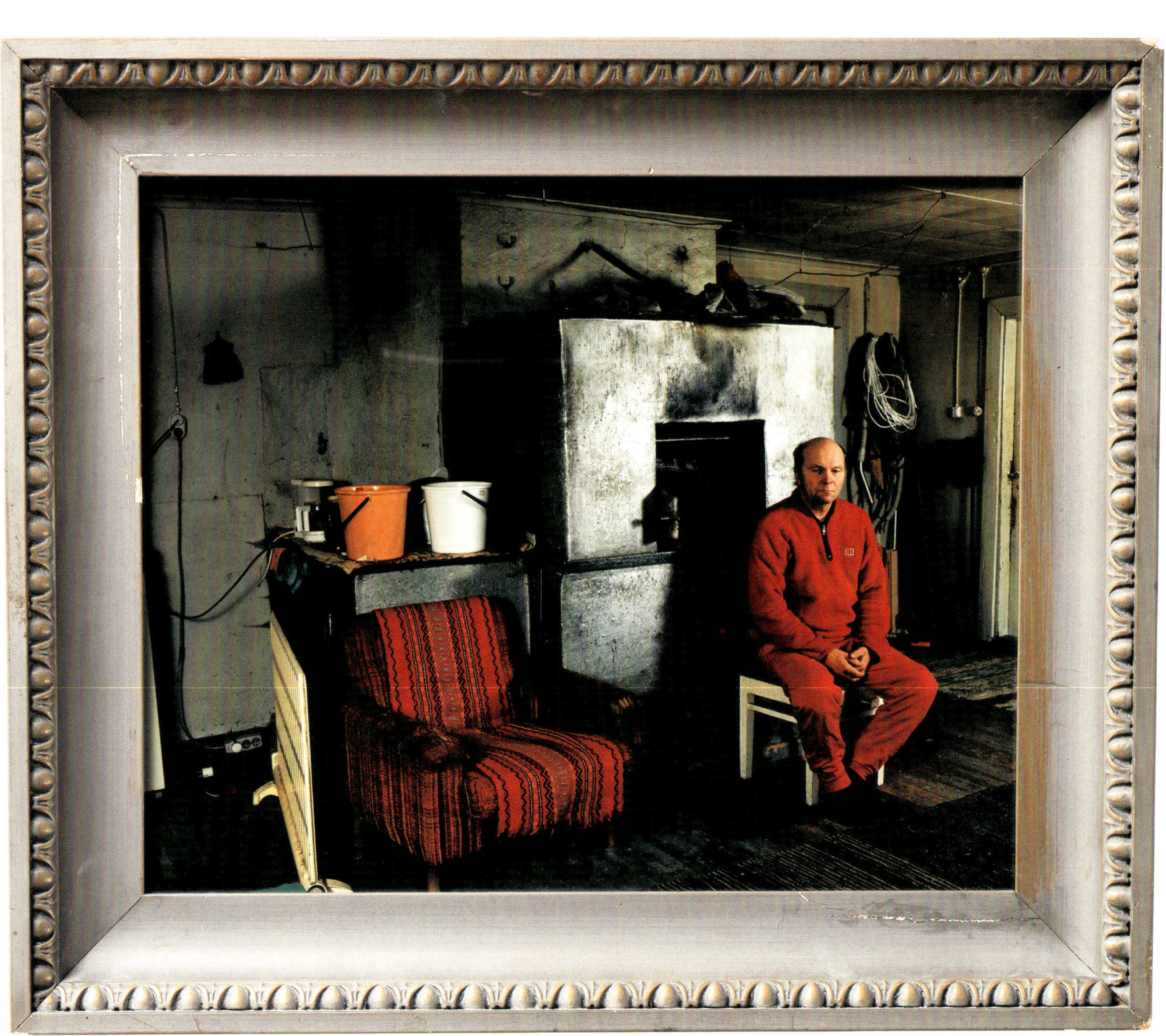

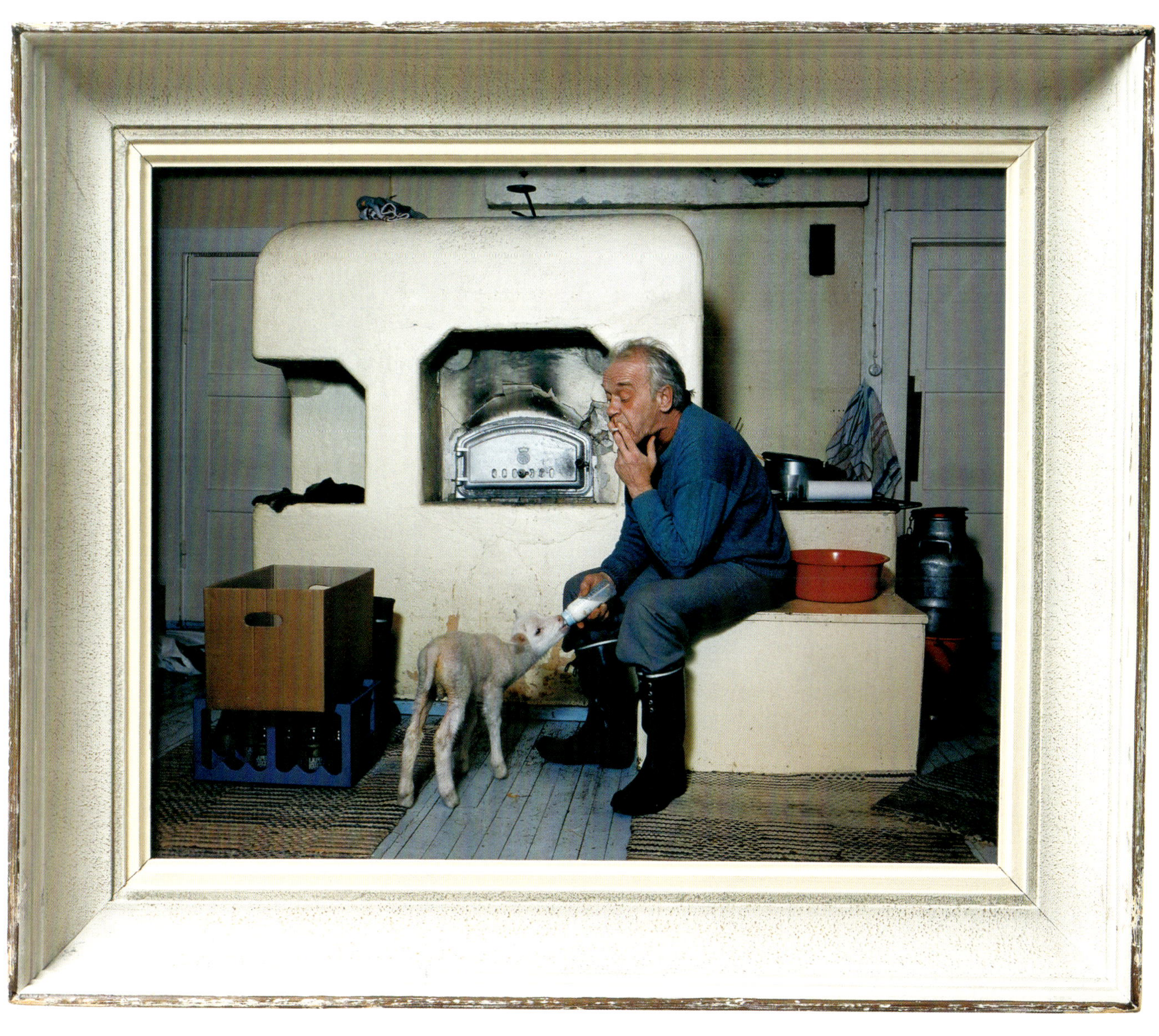

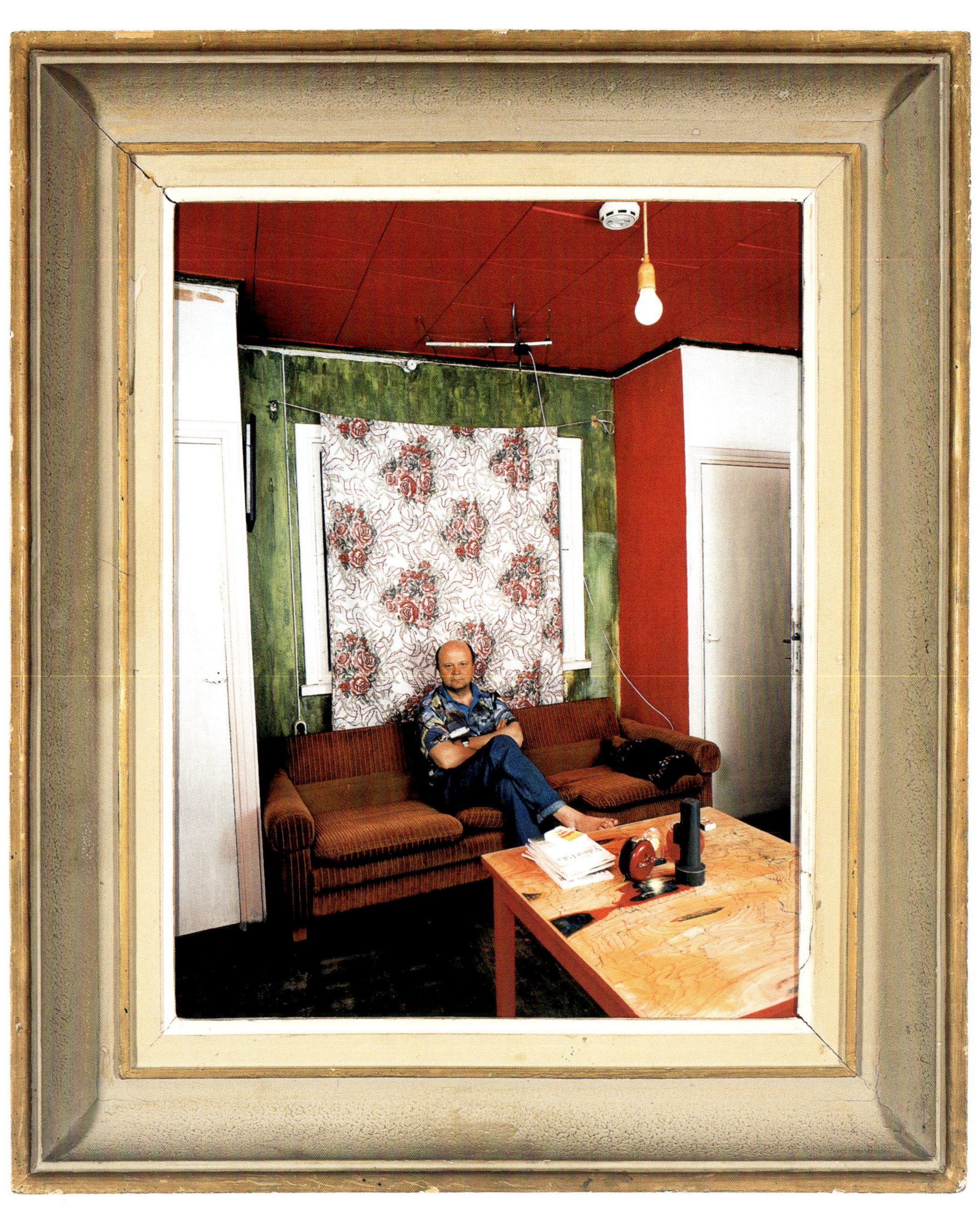

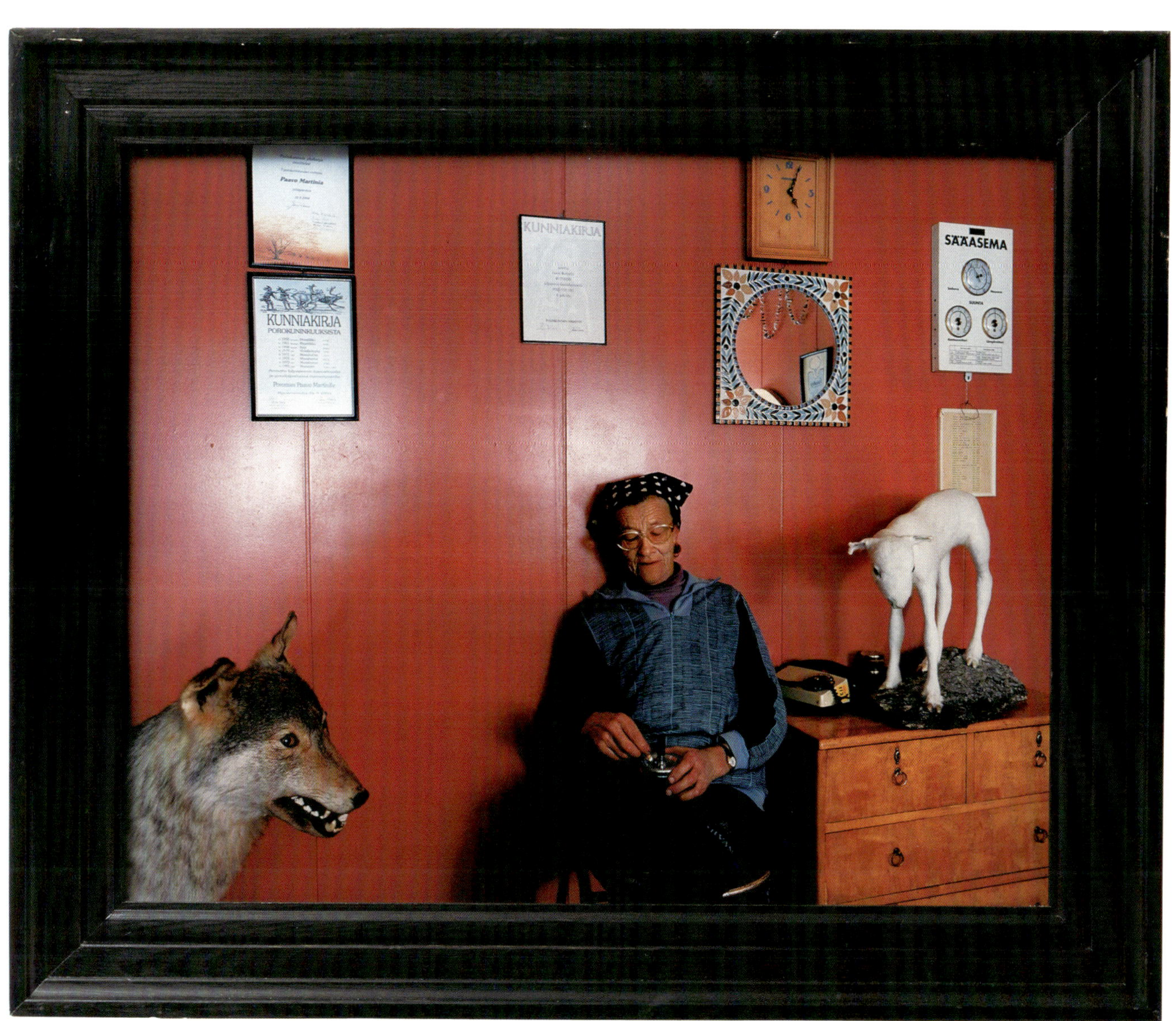

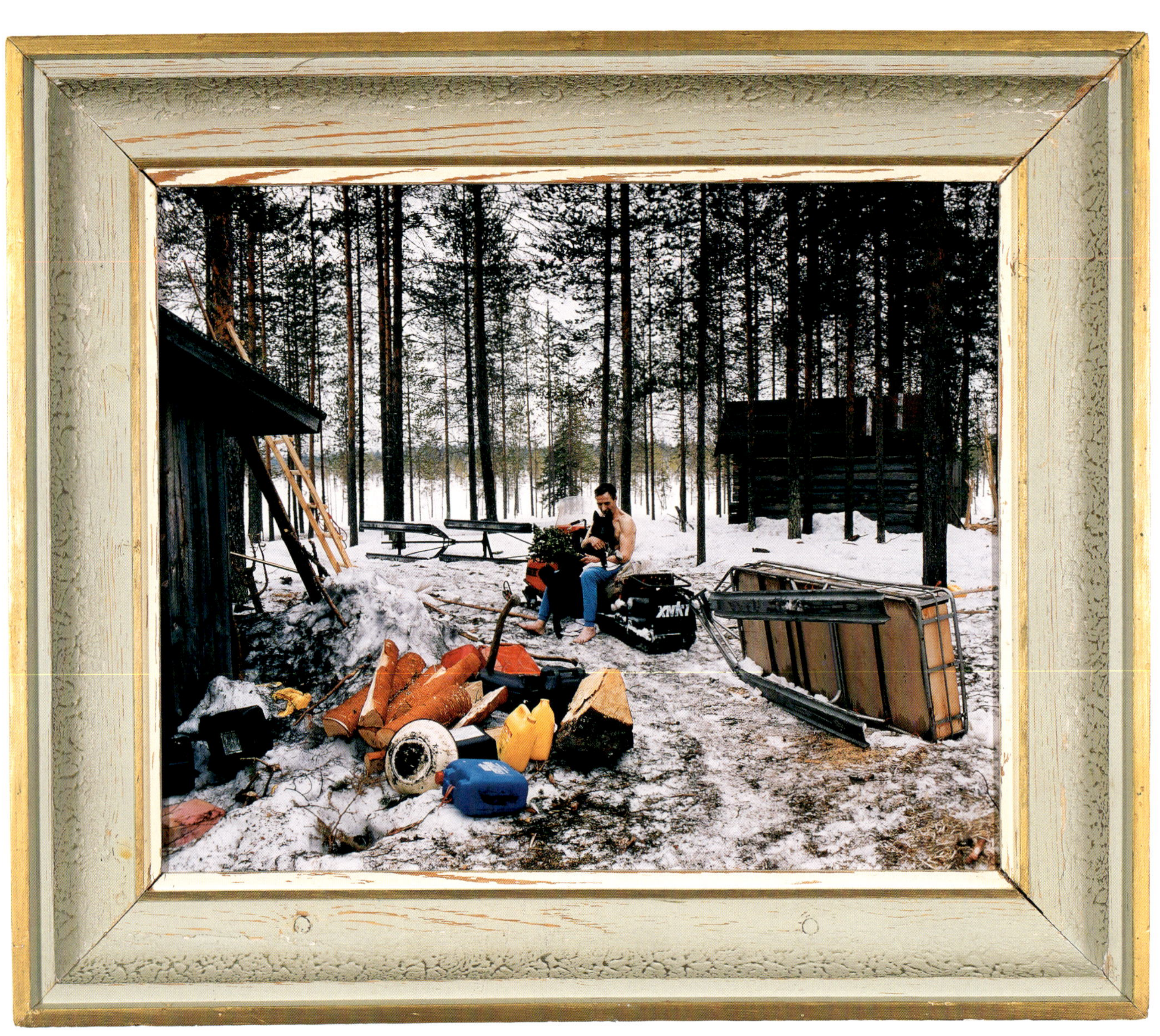

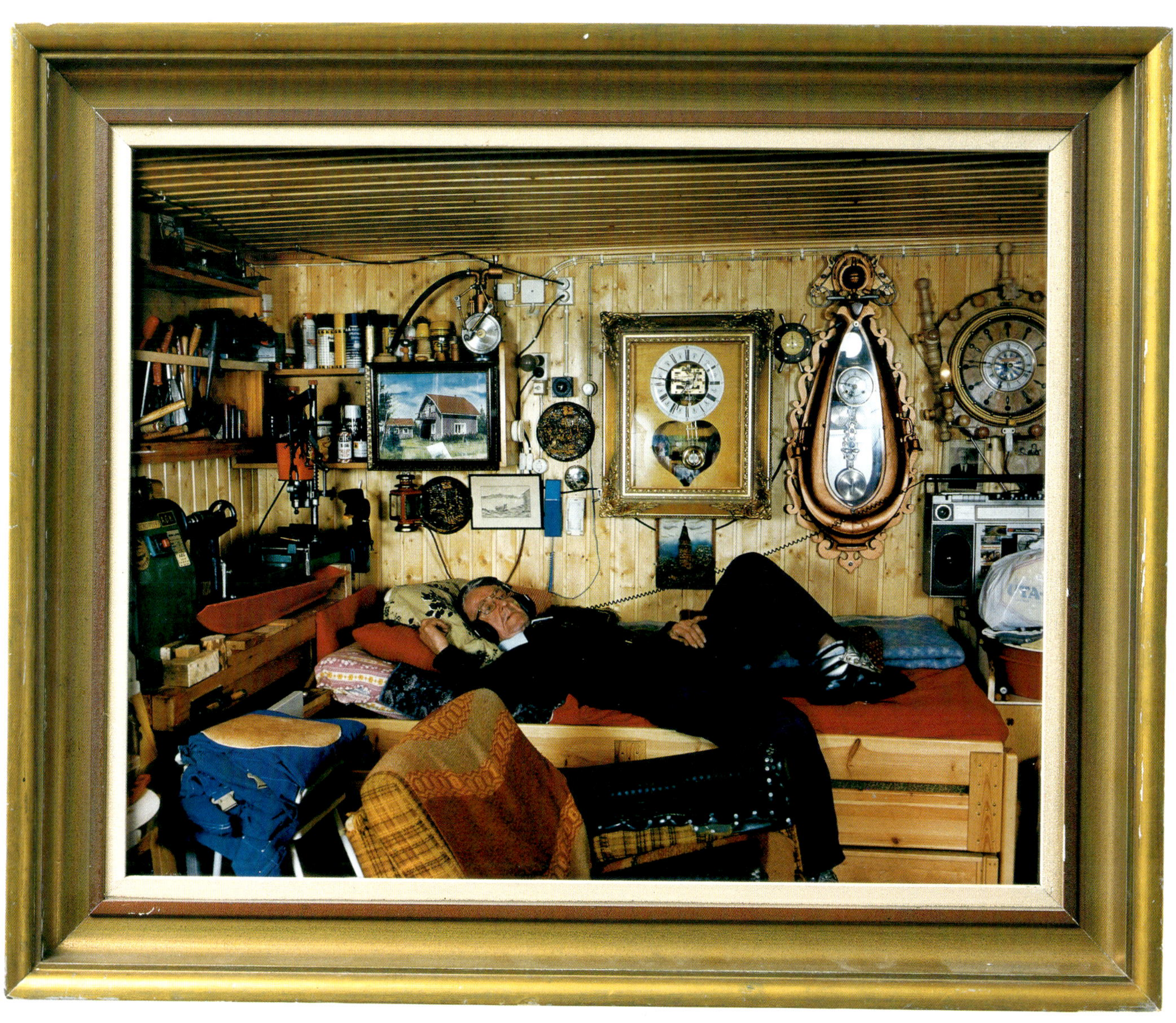

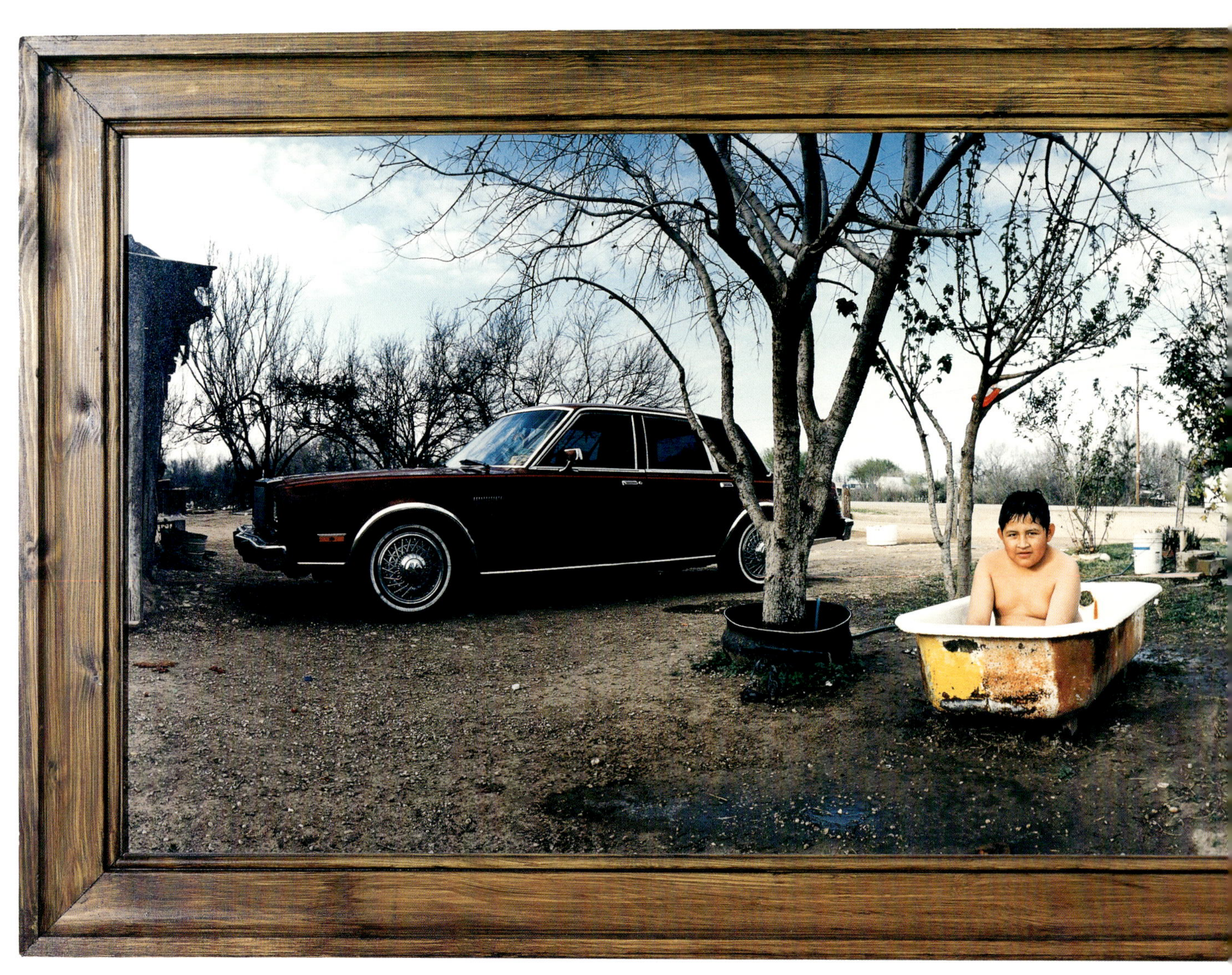

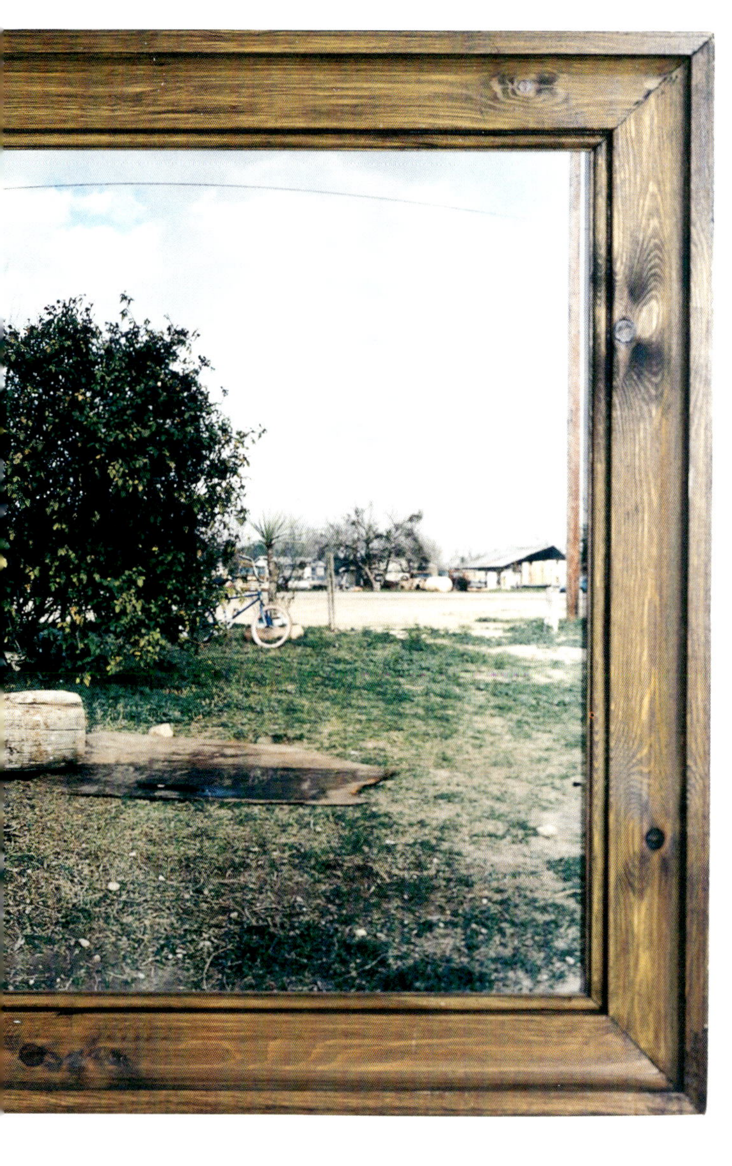

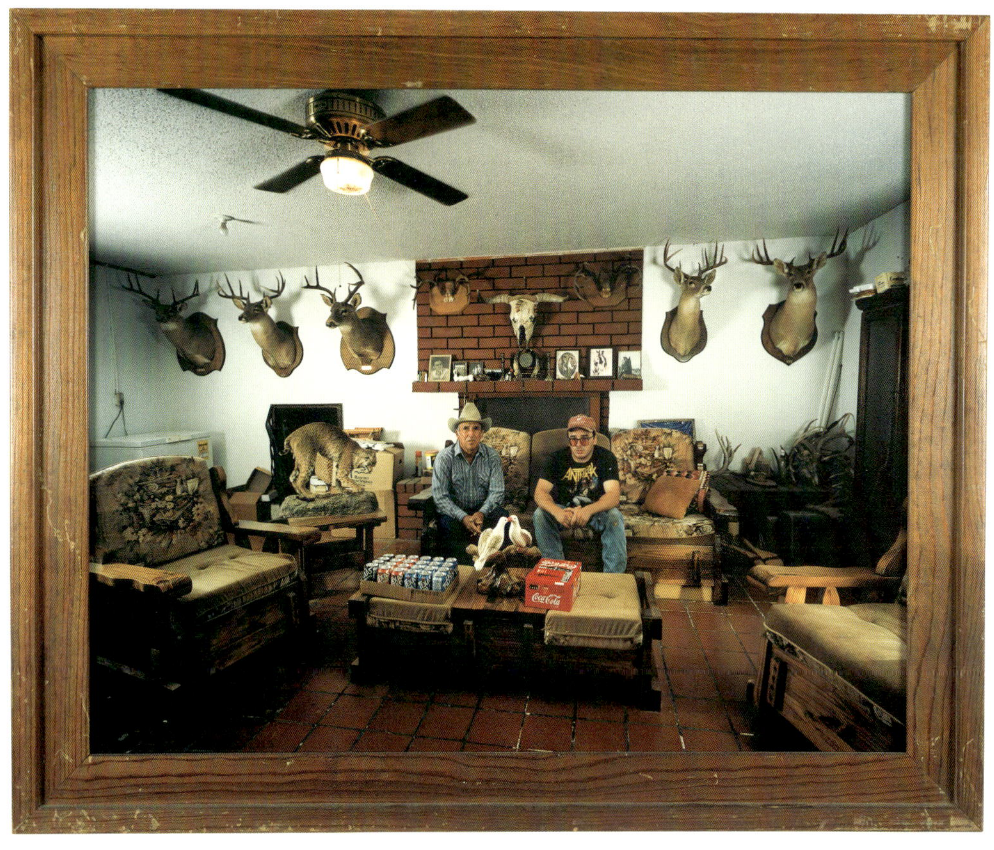

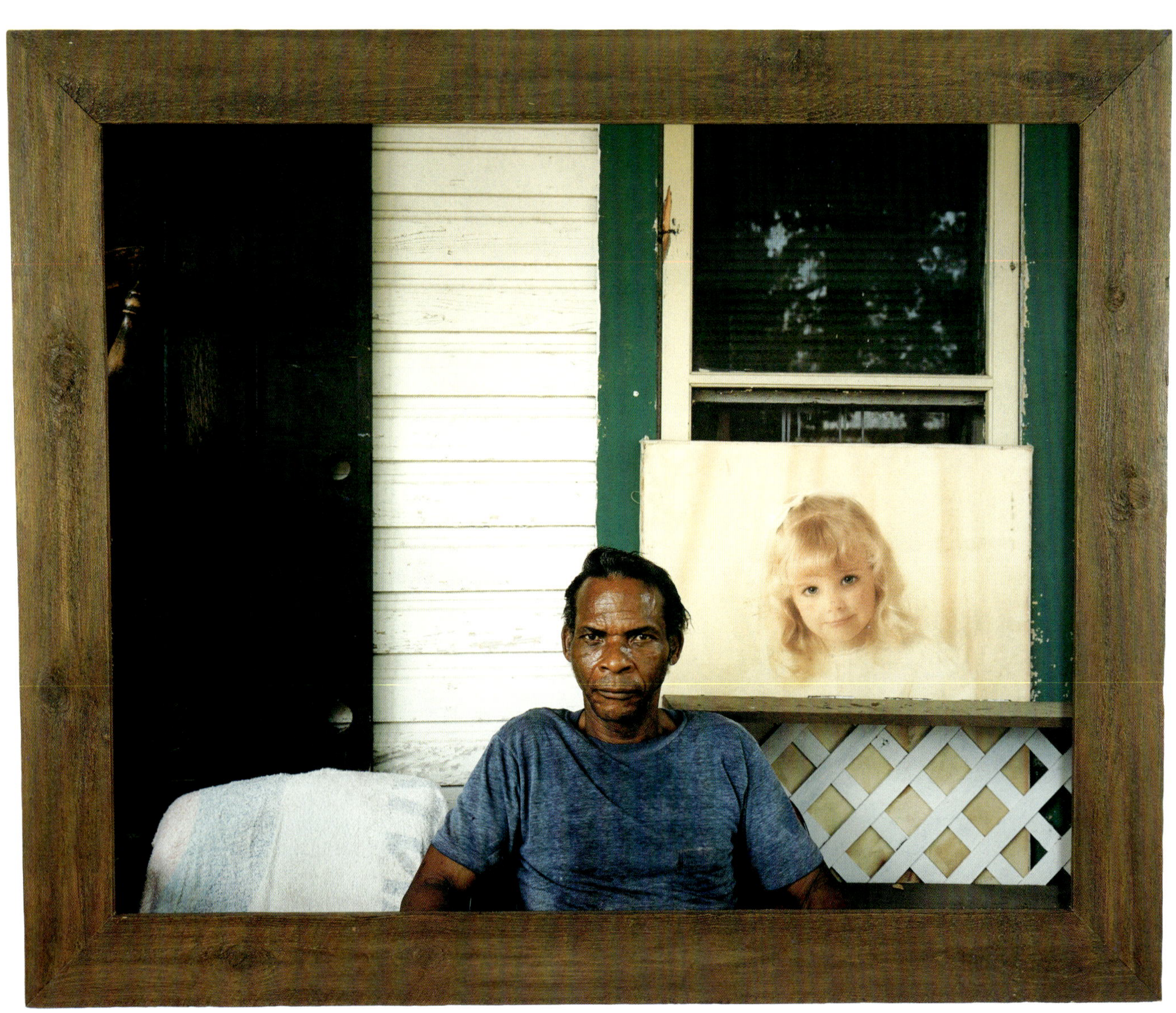

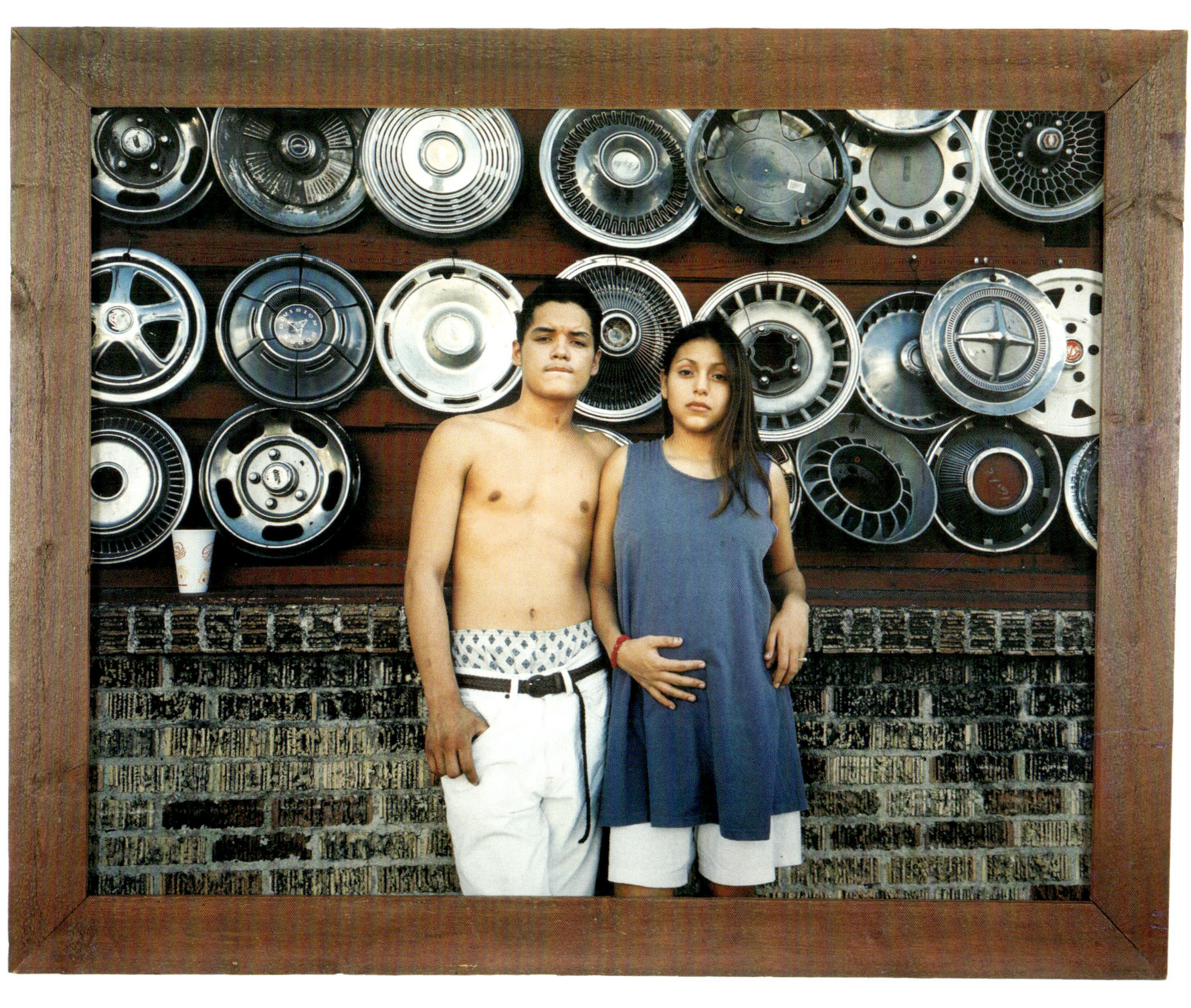

ugo **rondinone**

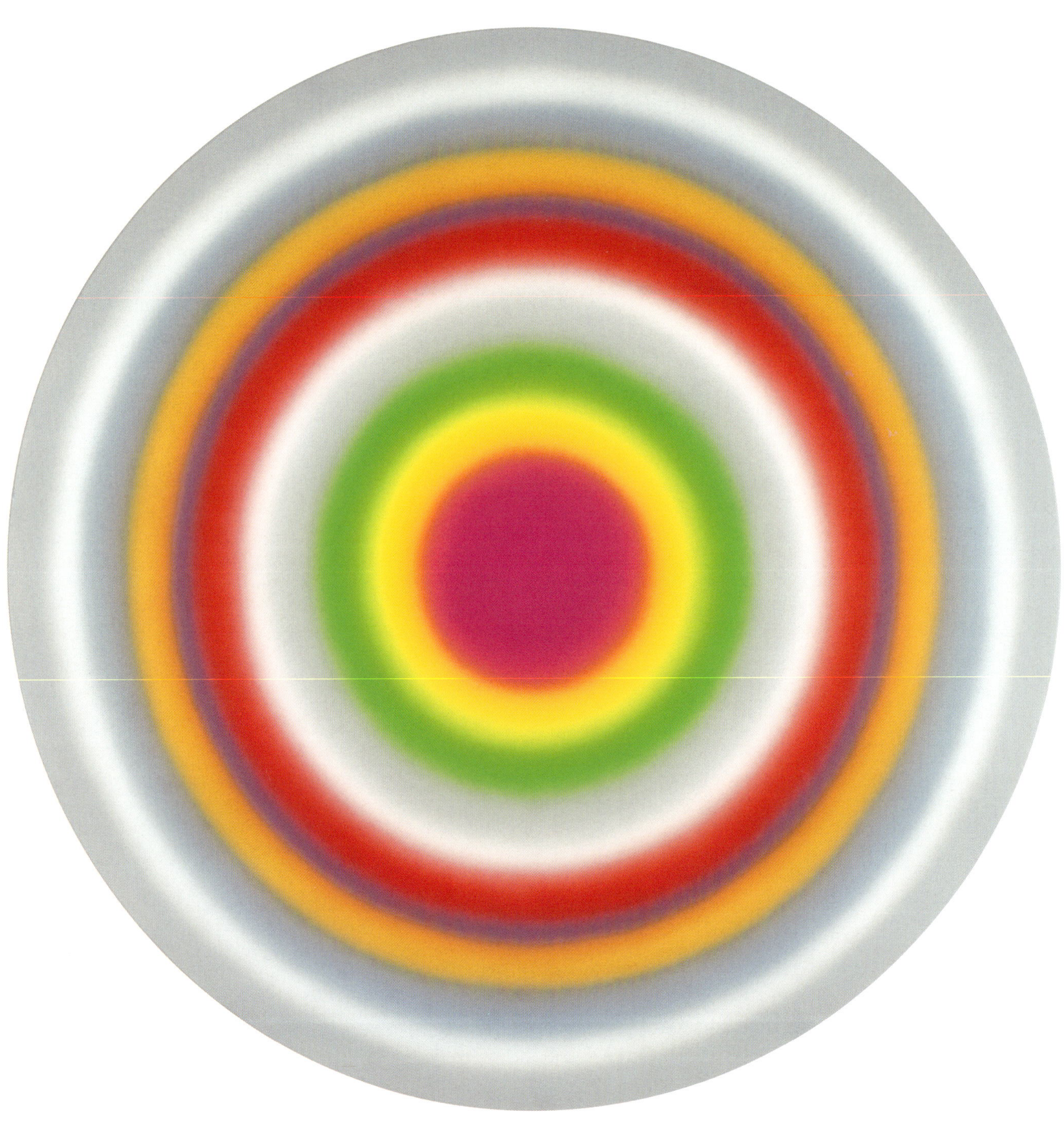

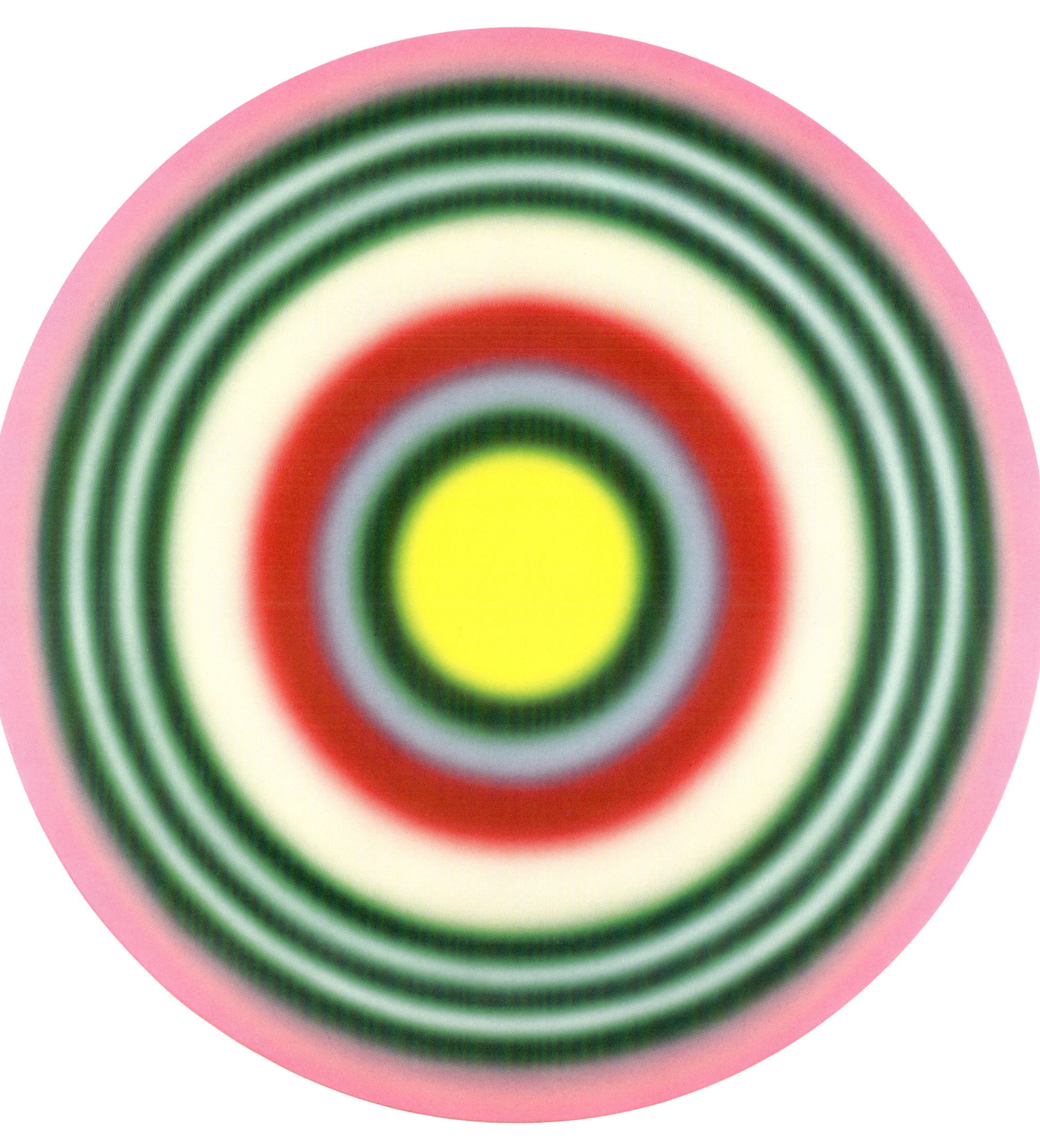

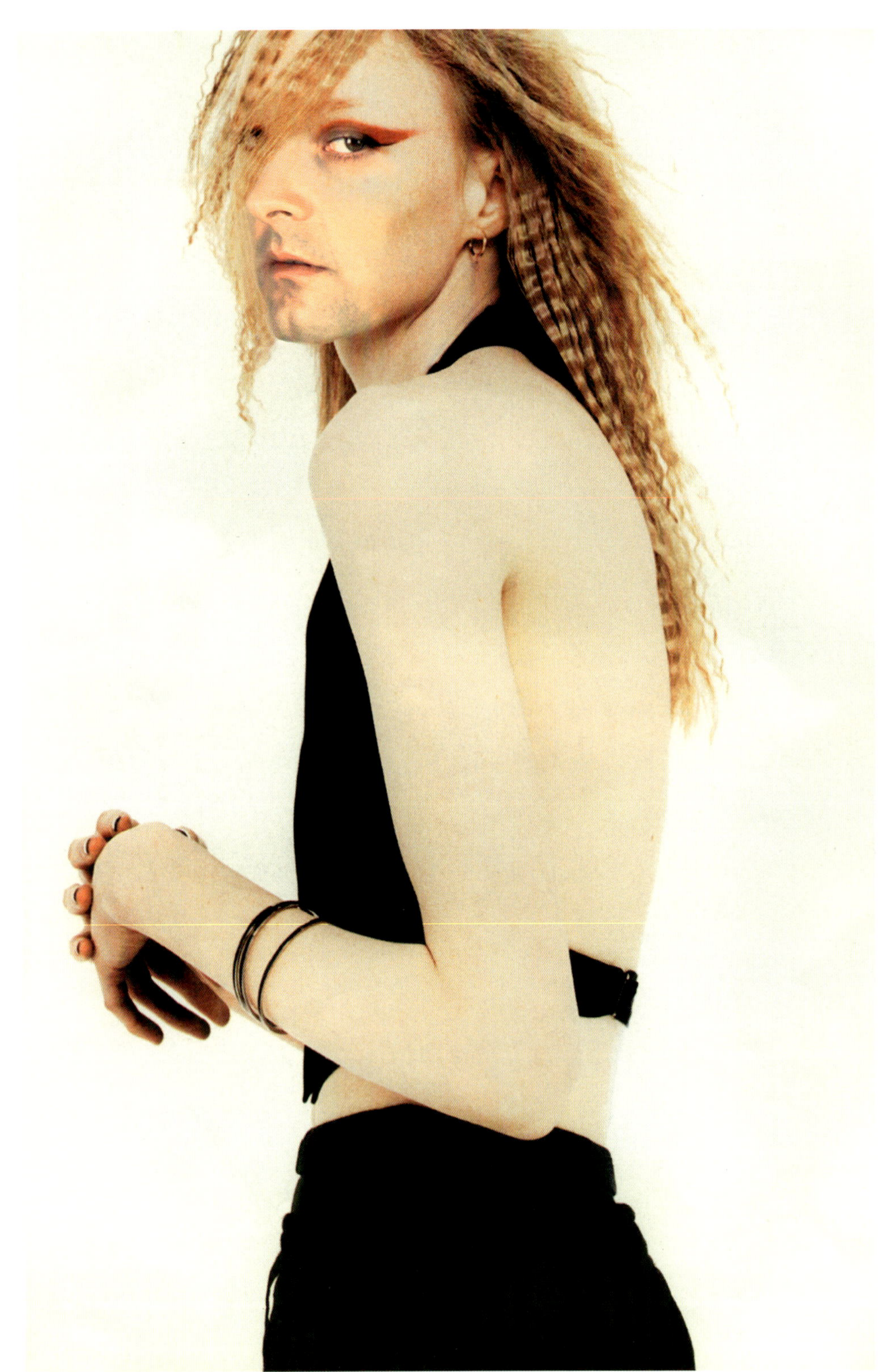

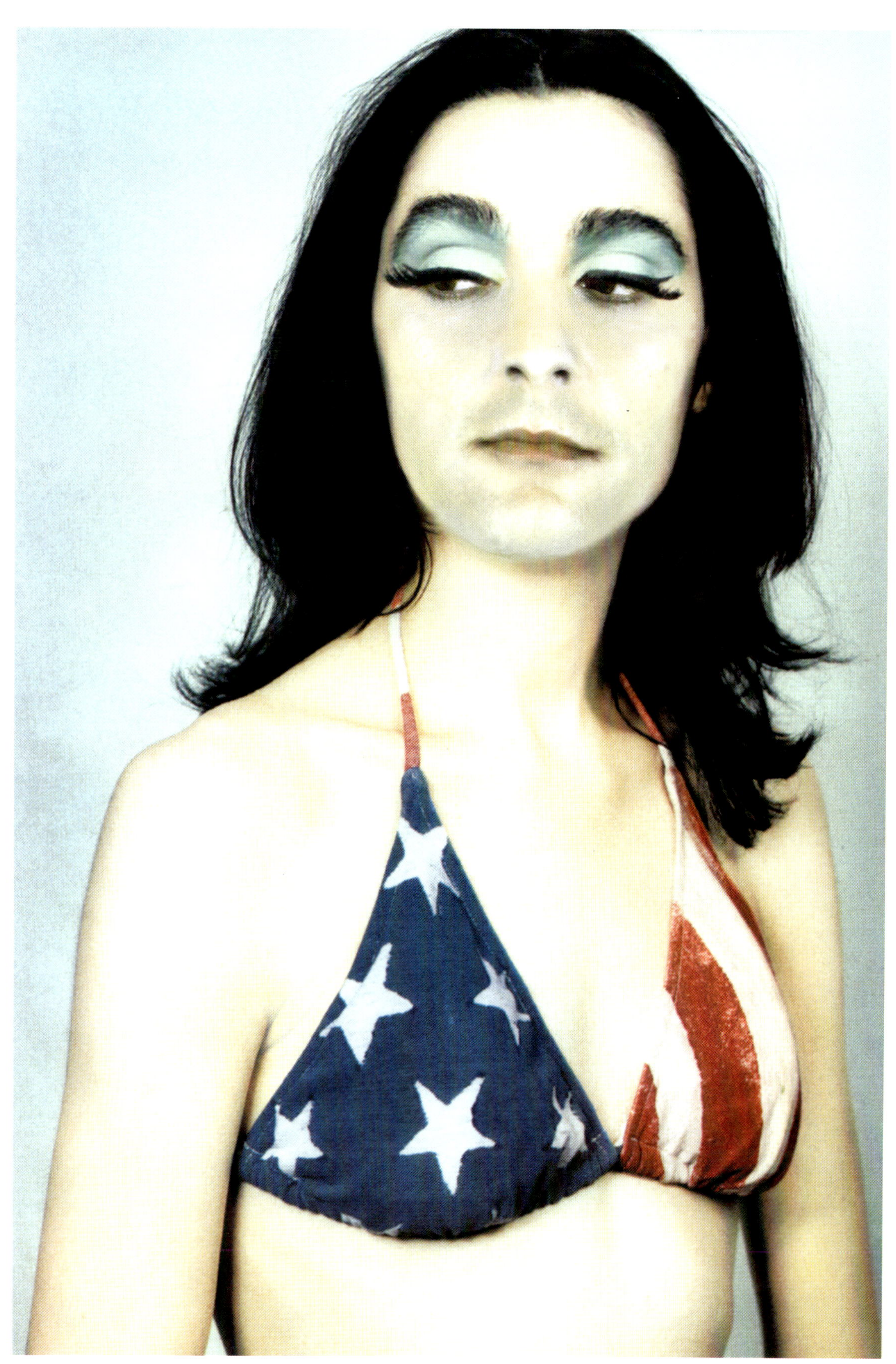

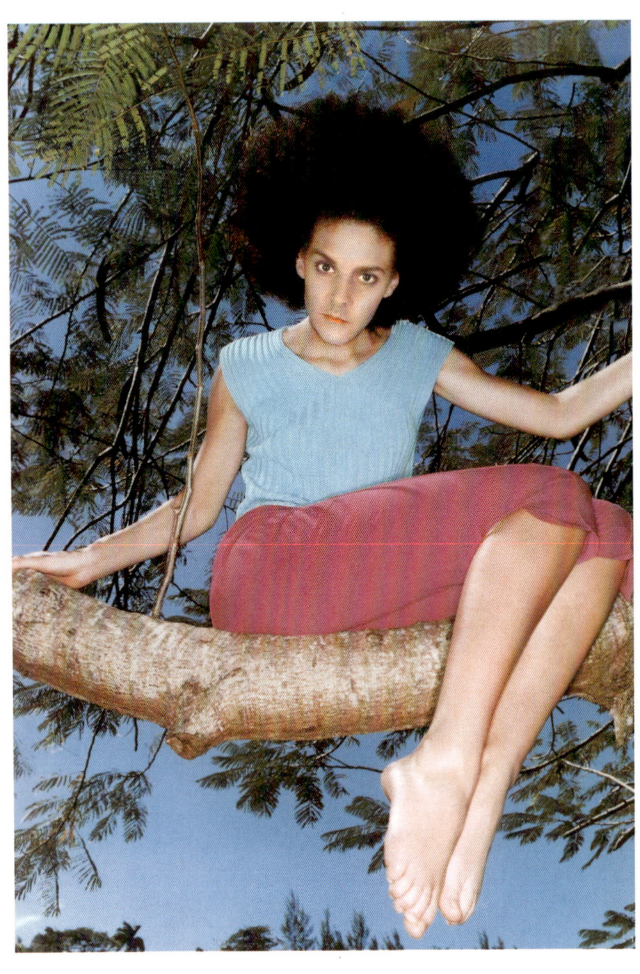

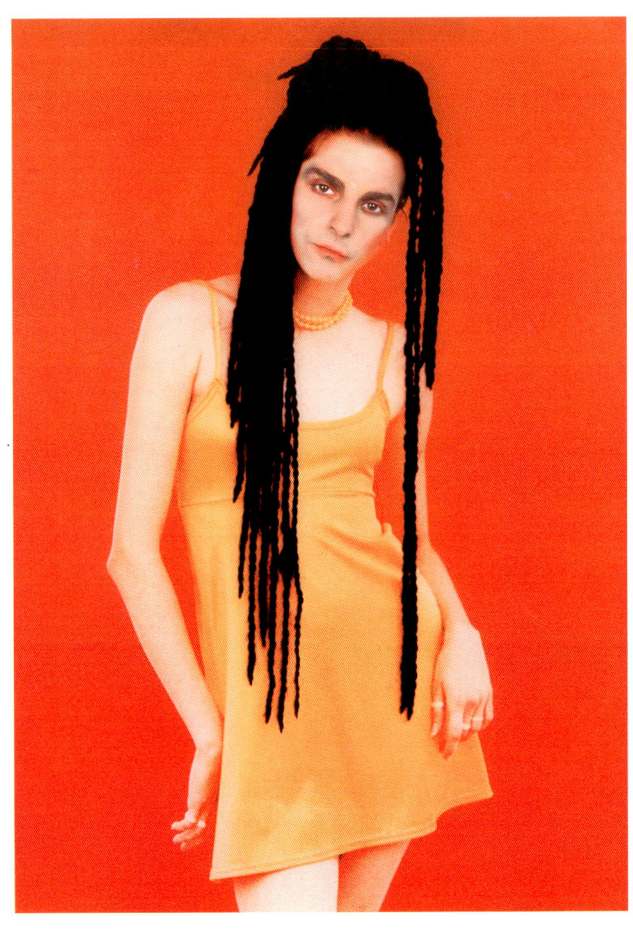

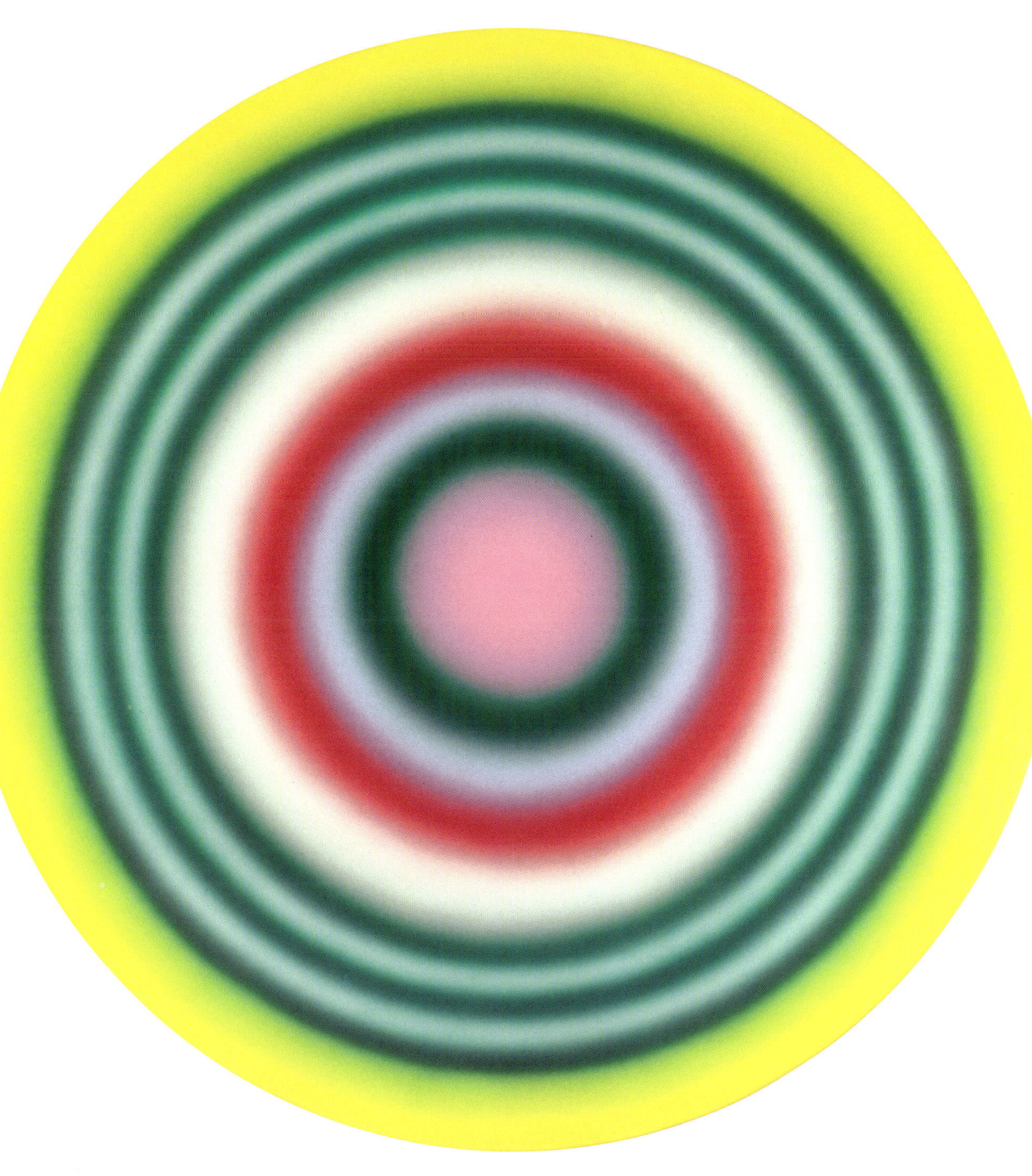

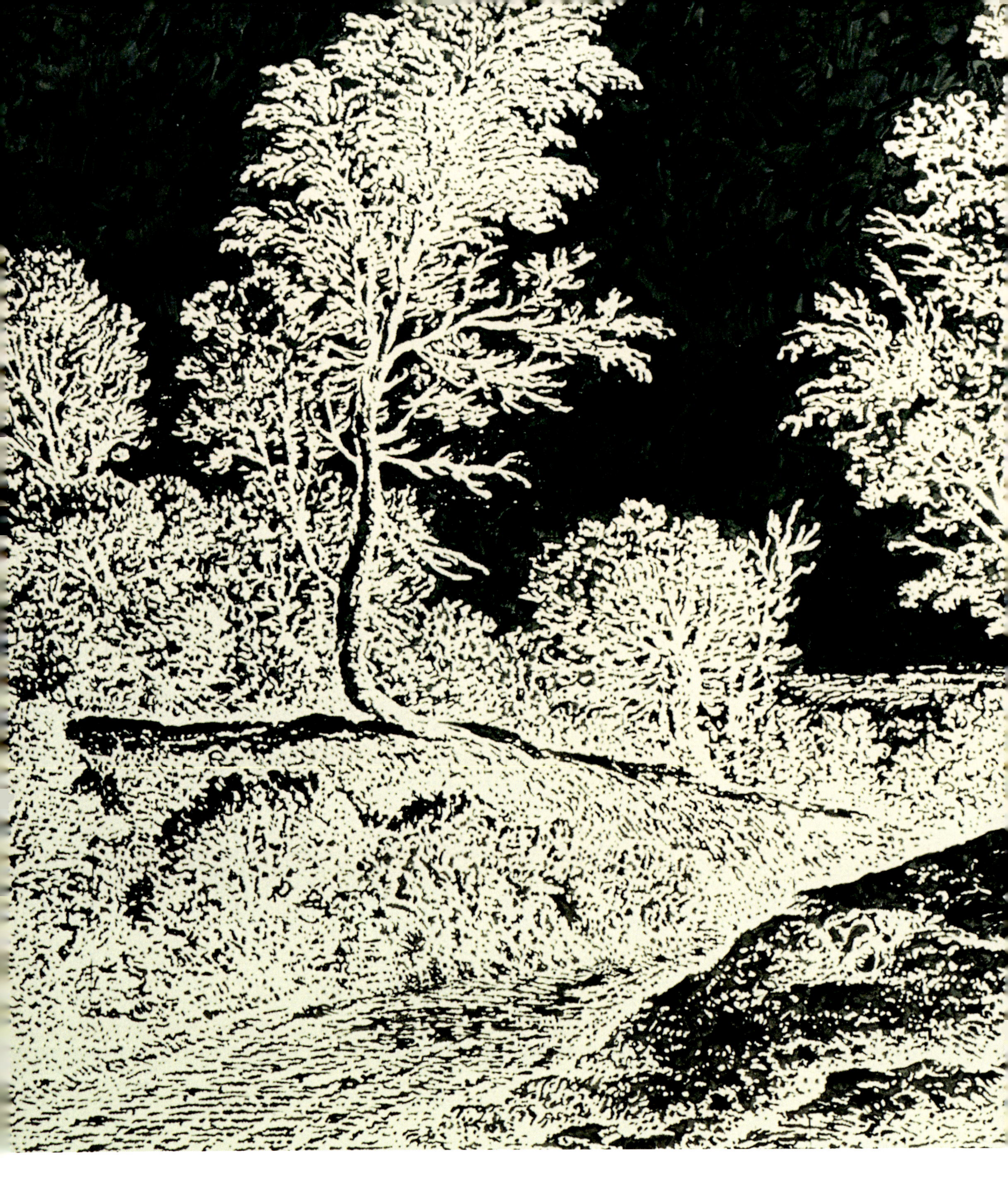

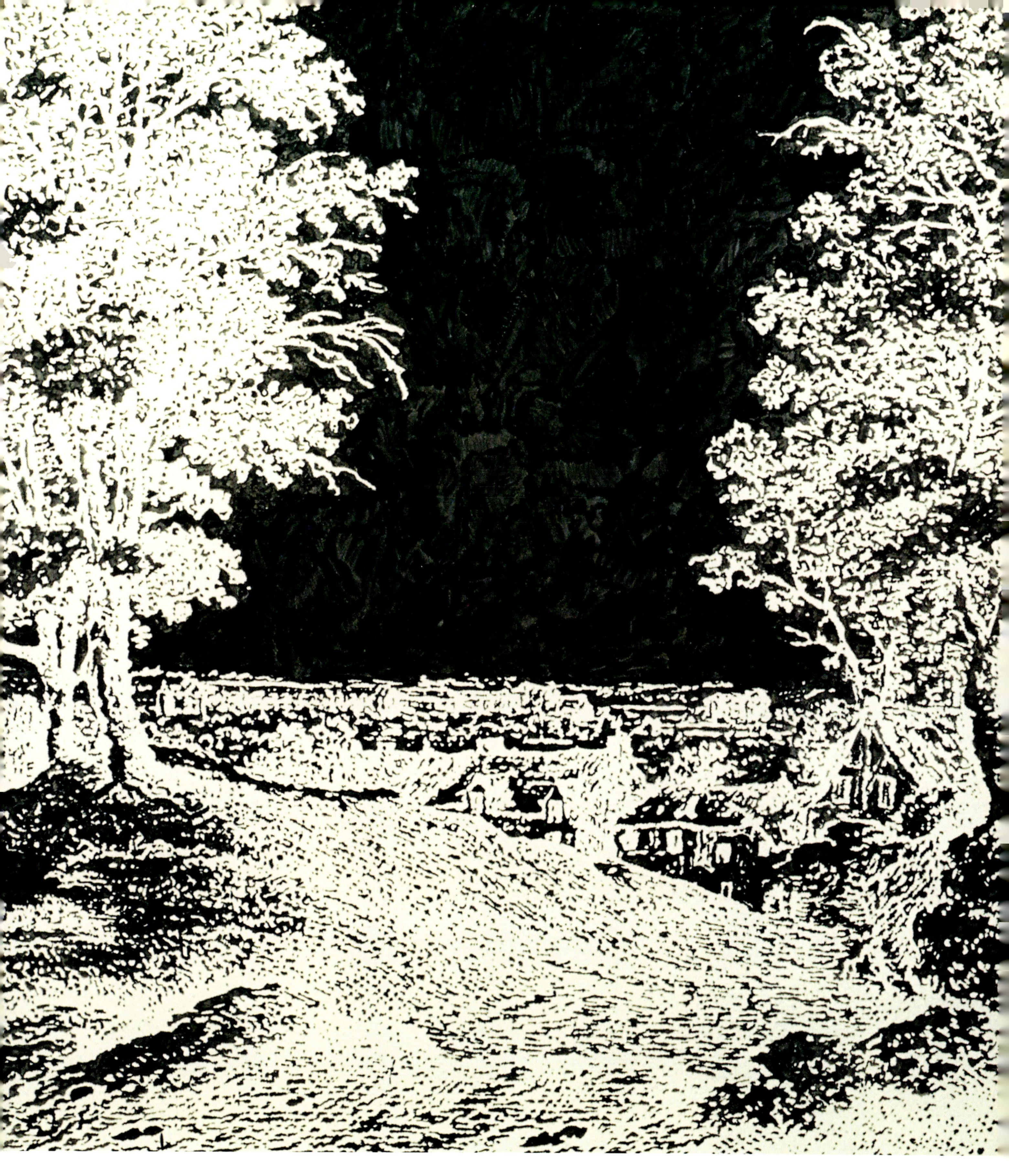

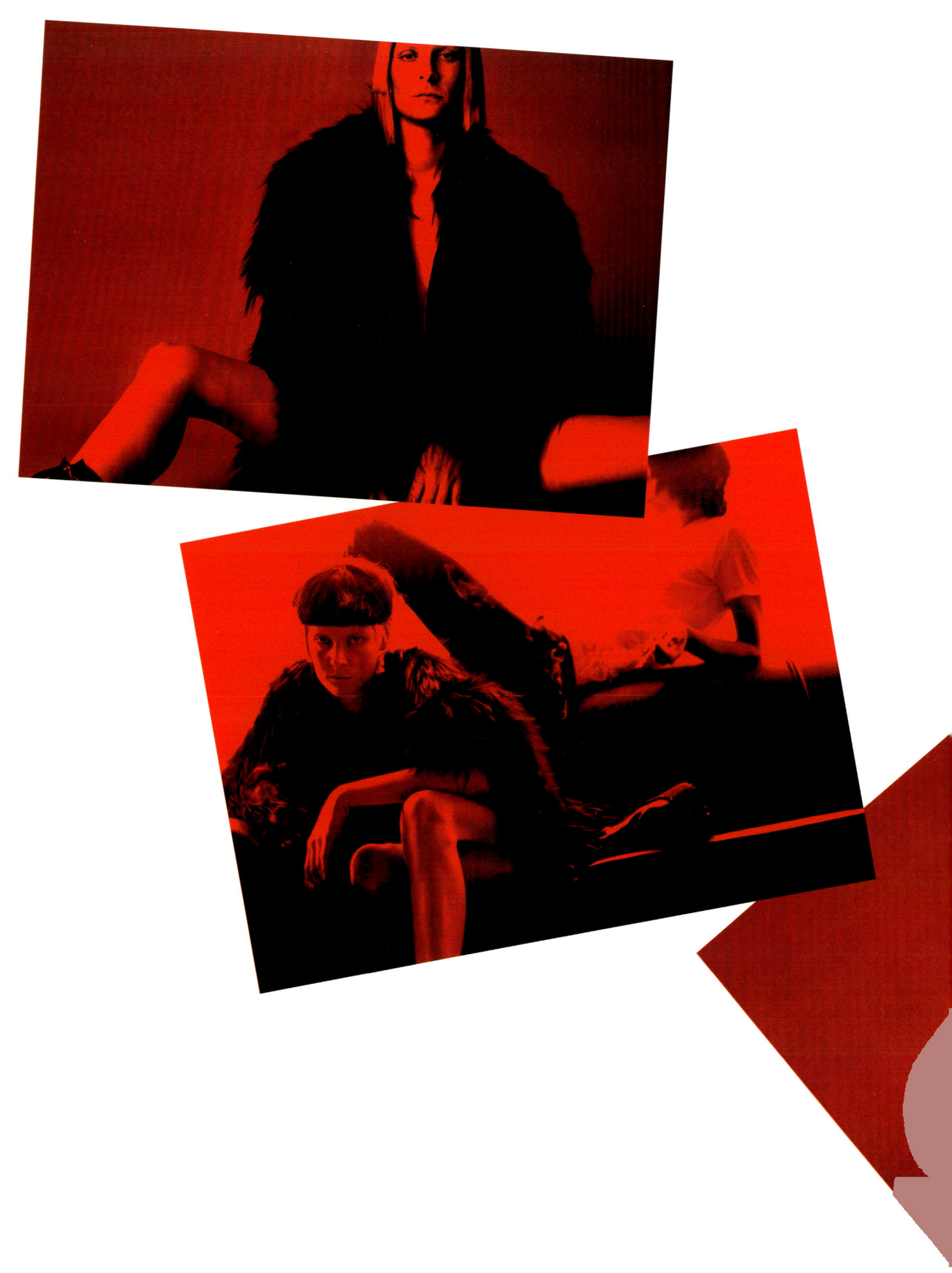

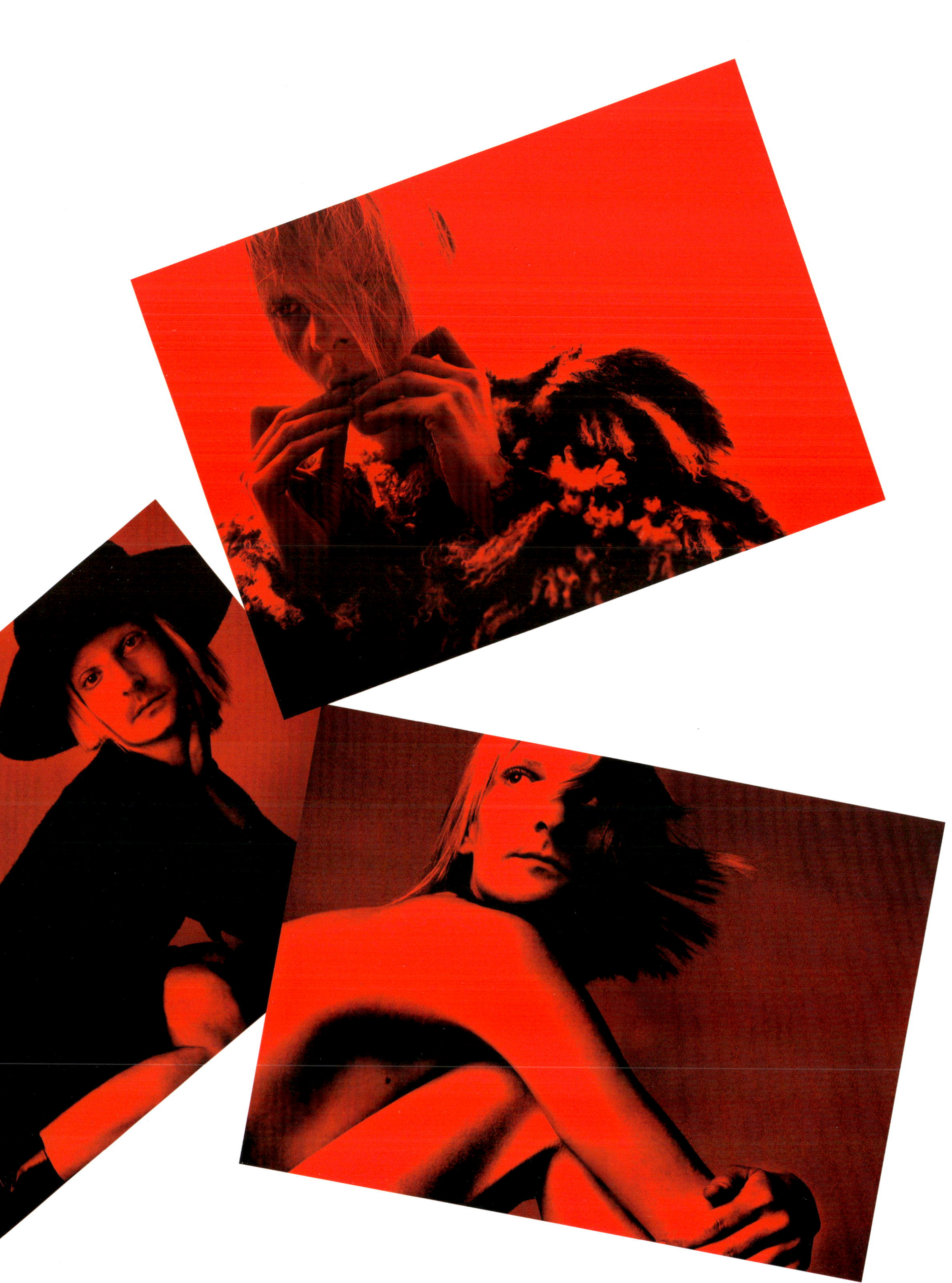

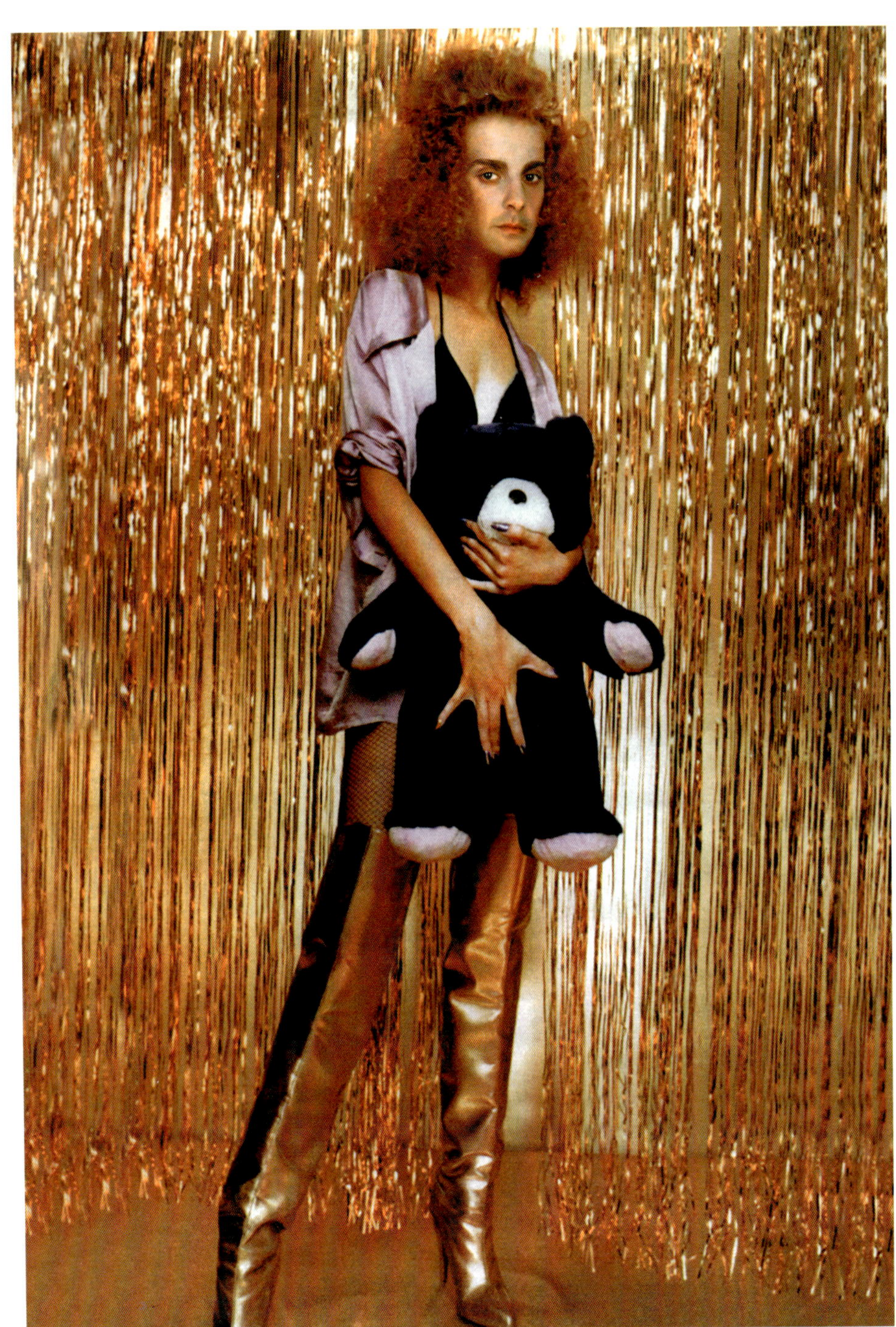

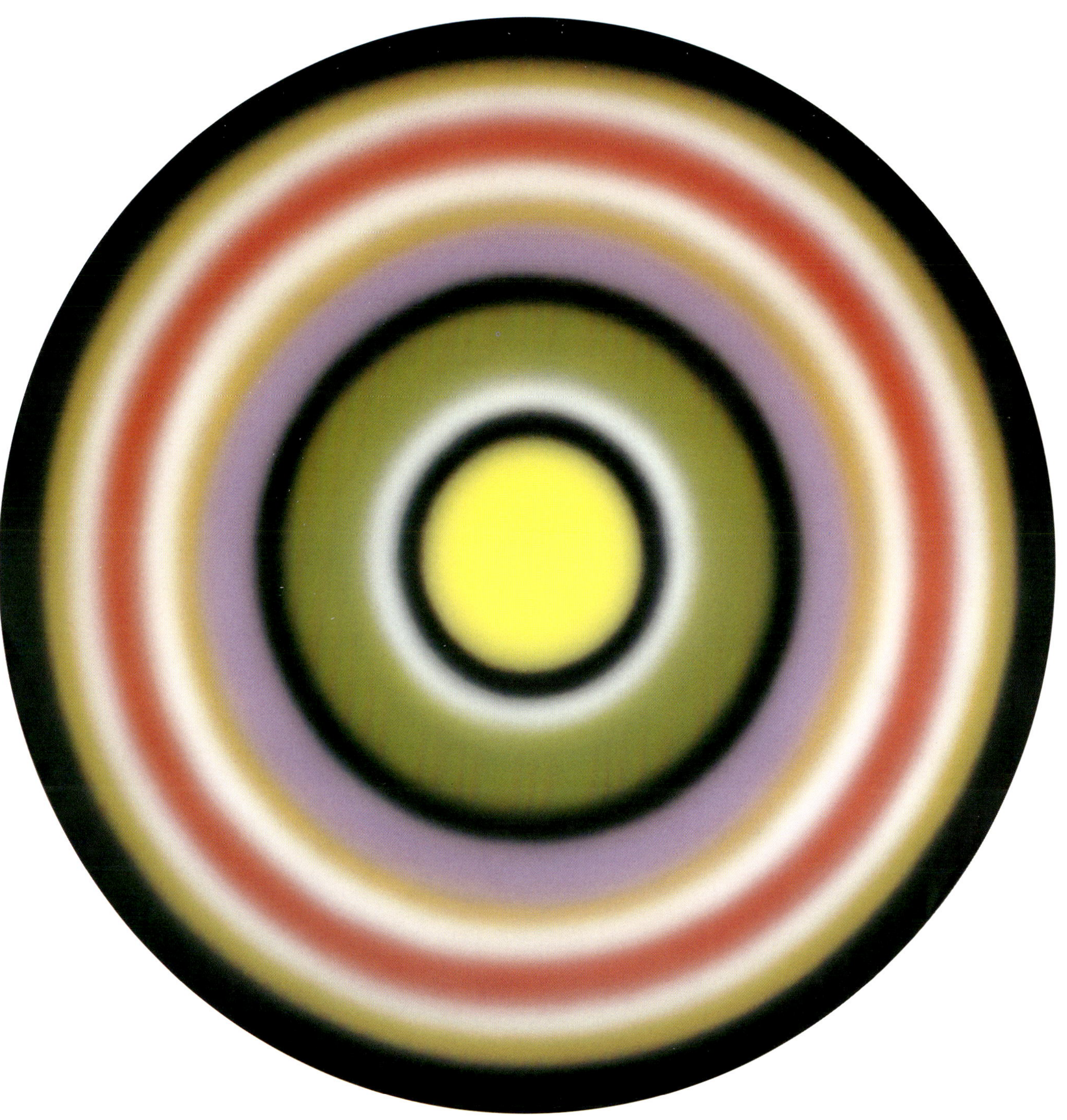

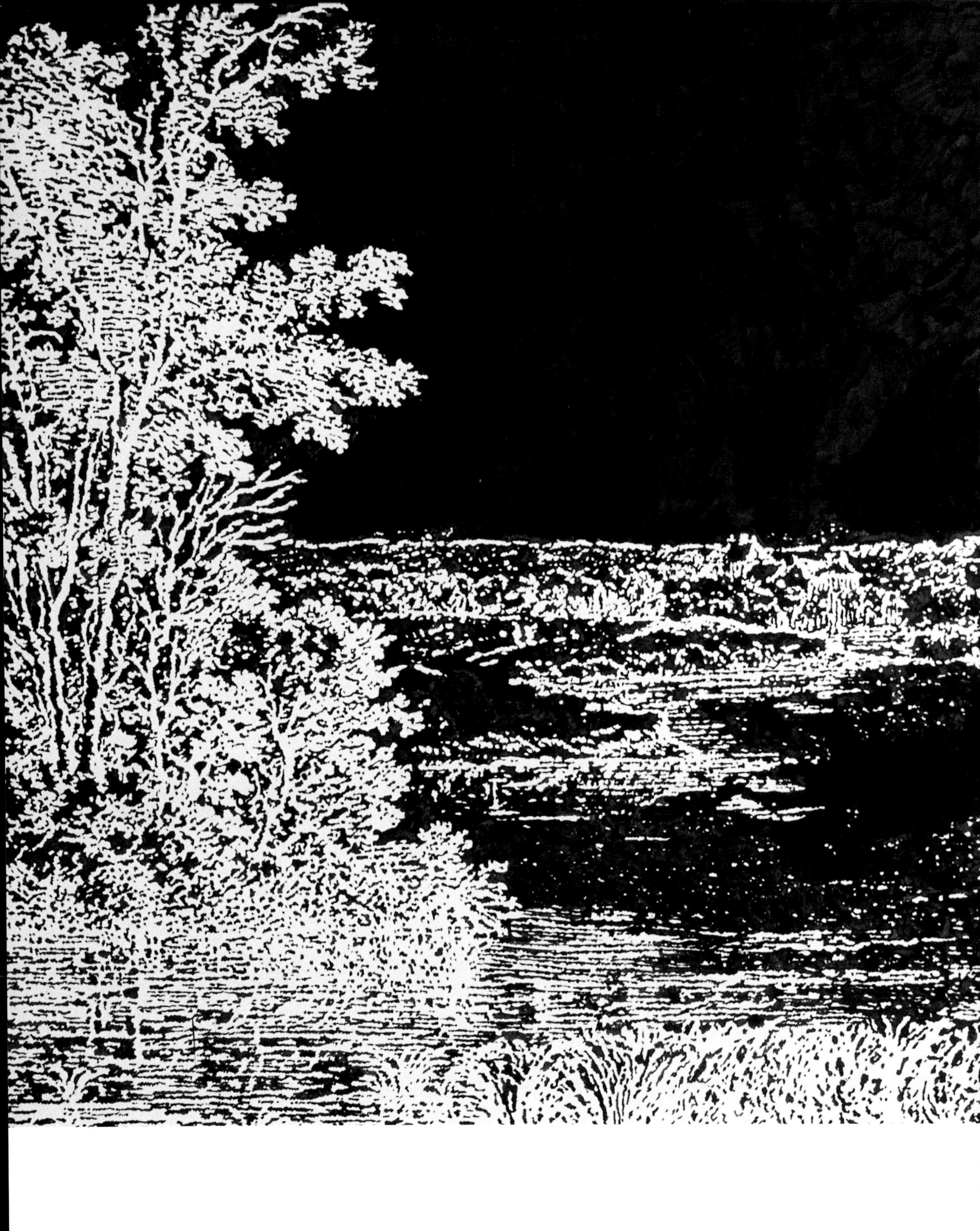

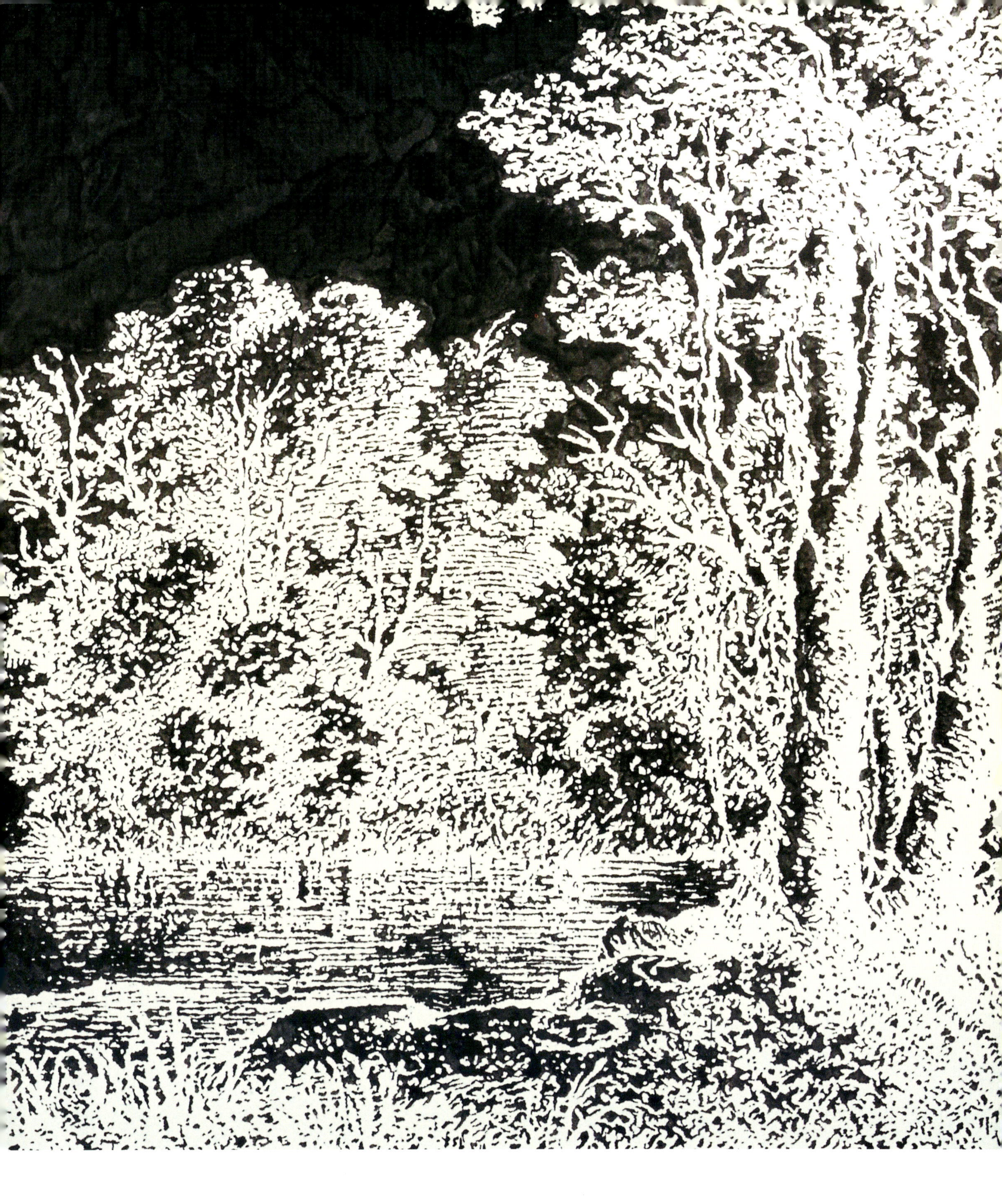

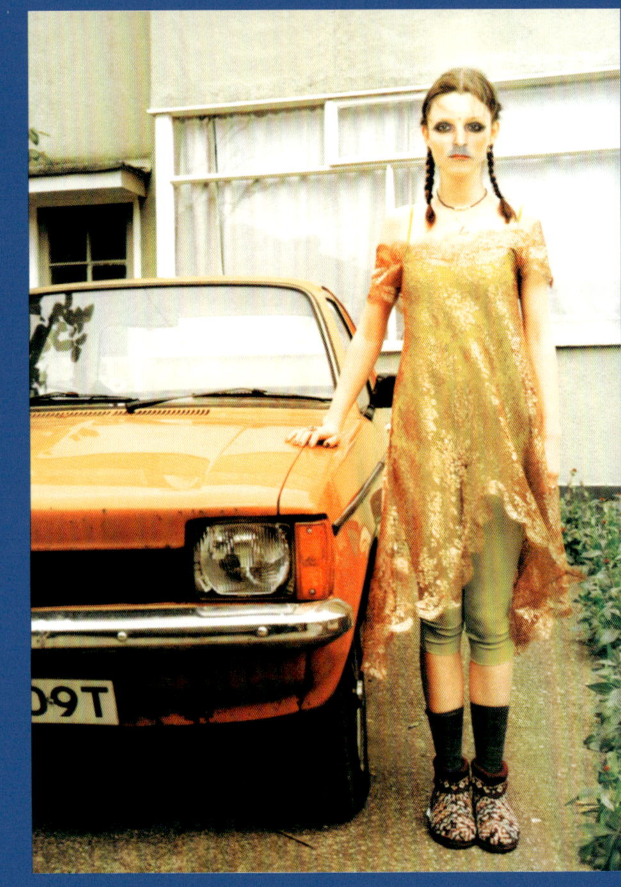
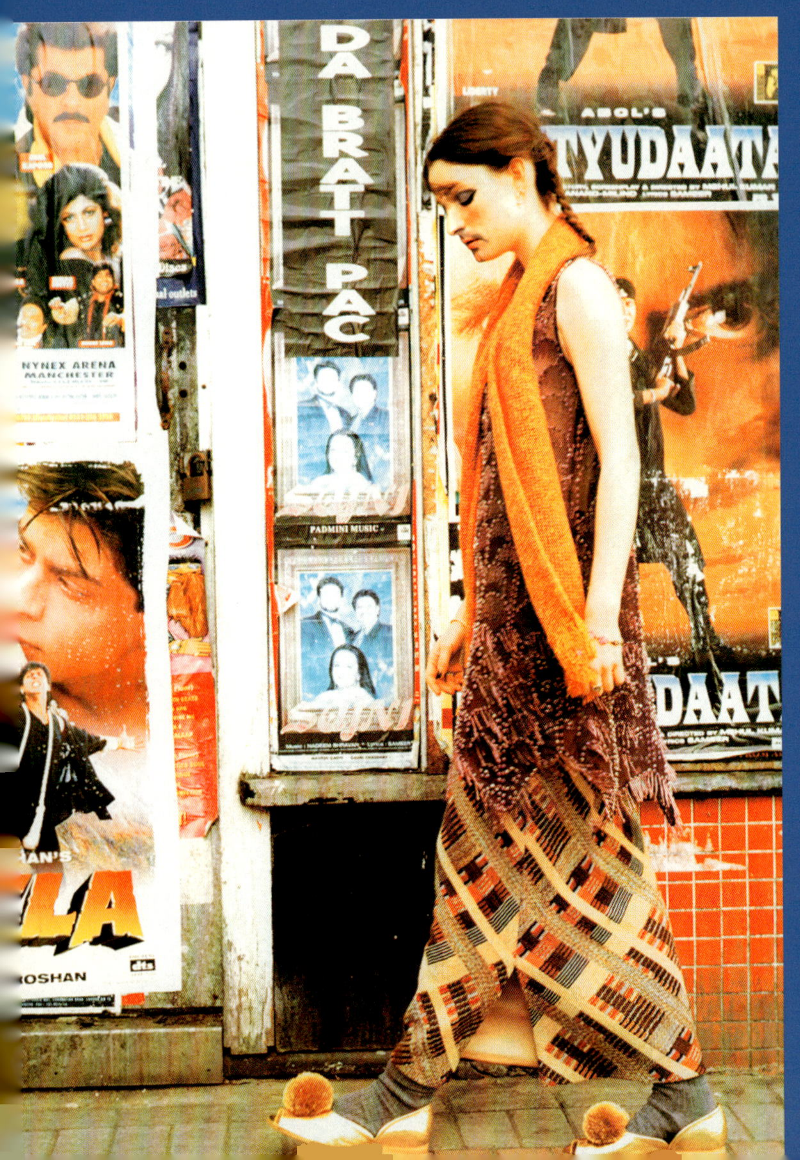
DA BRAT PAC
TYUDAATA
NYNEX ARENA
MANCHESTER
PADMINI MUSIC
DAATA
ROSHAN

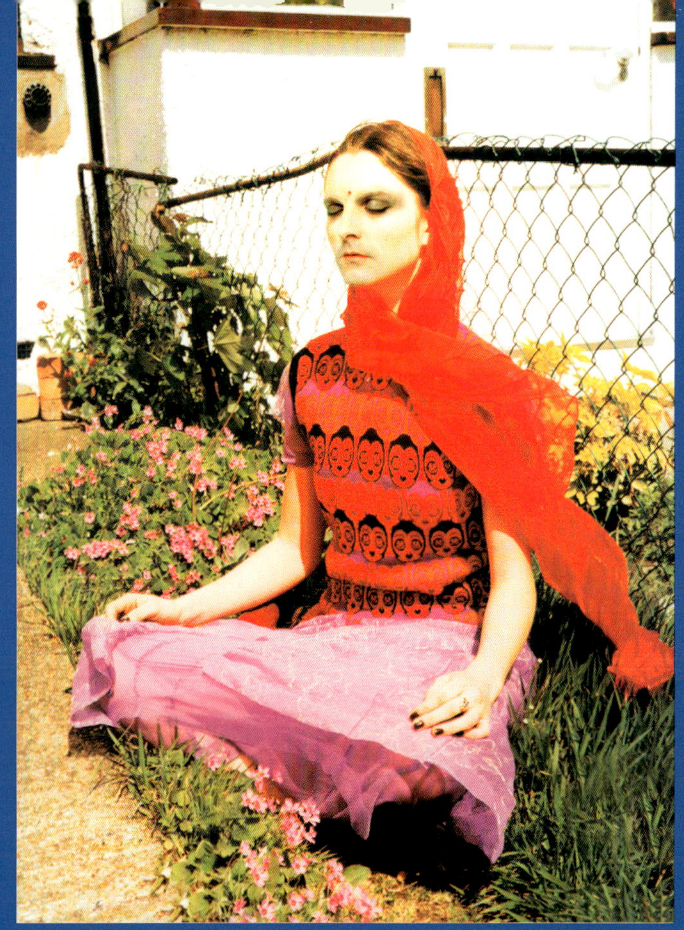

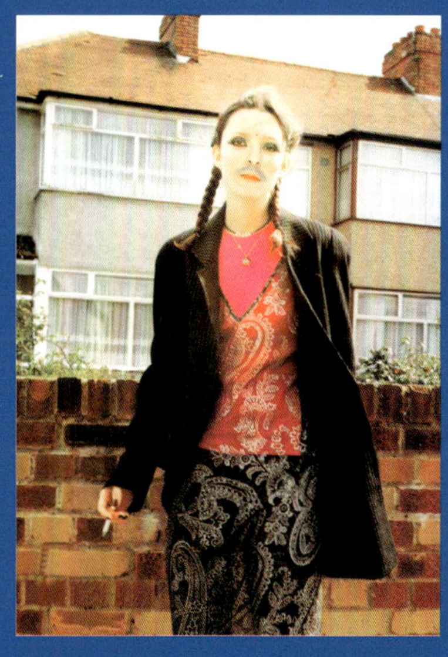

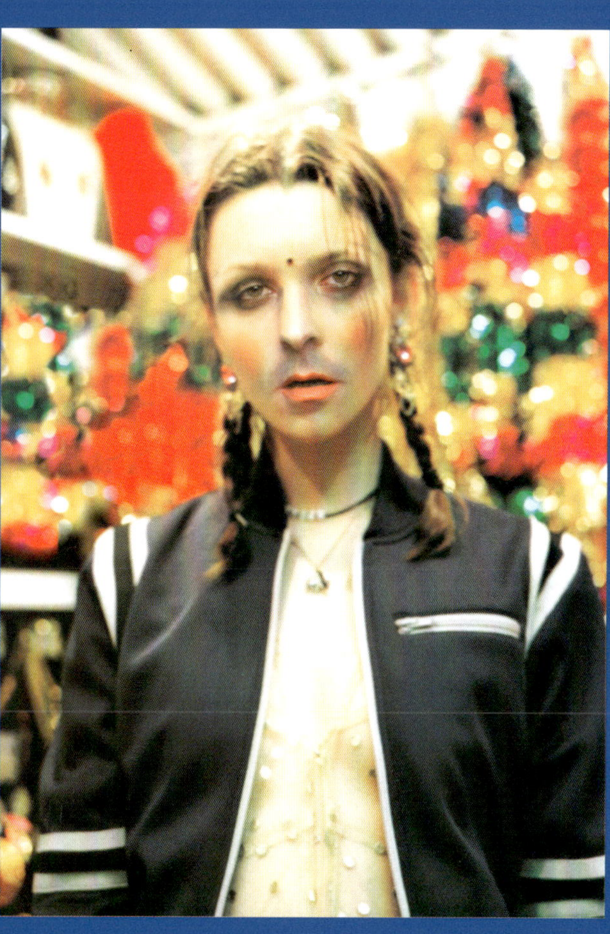

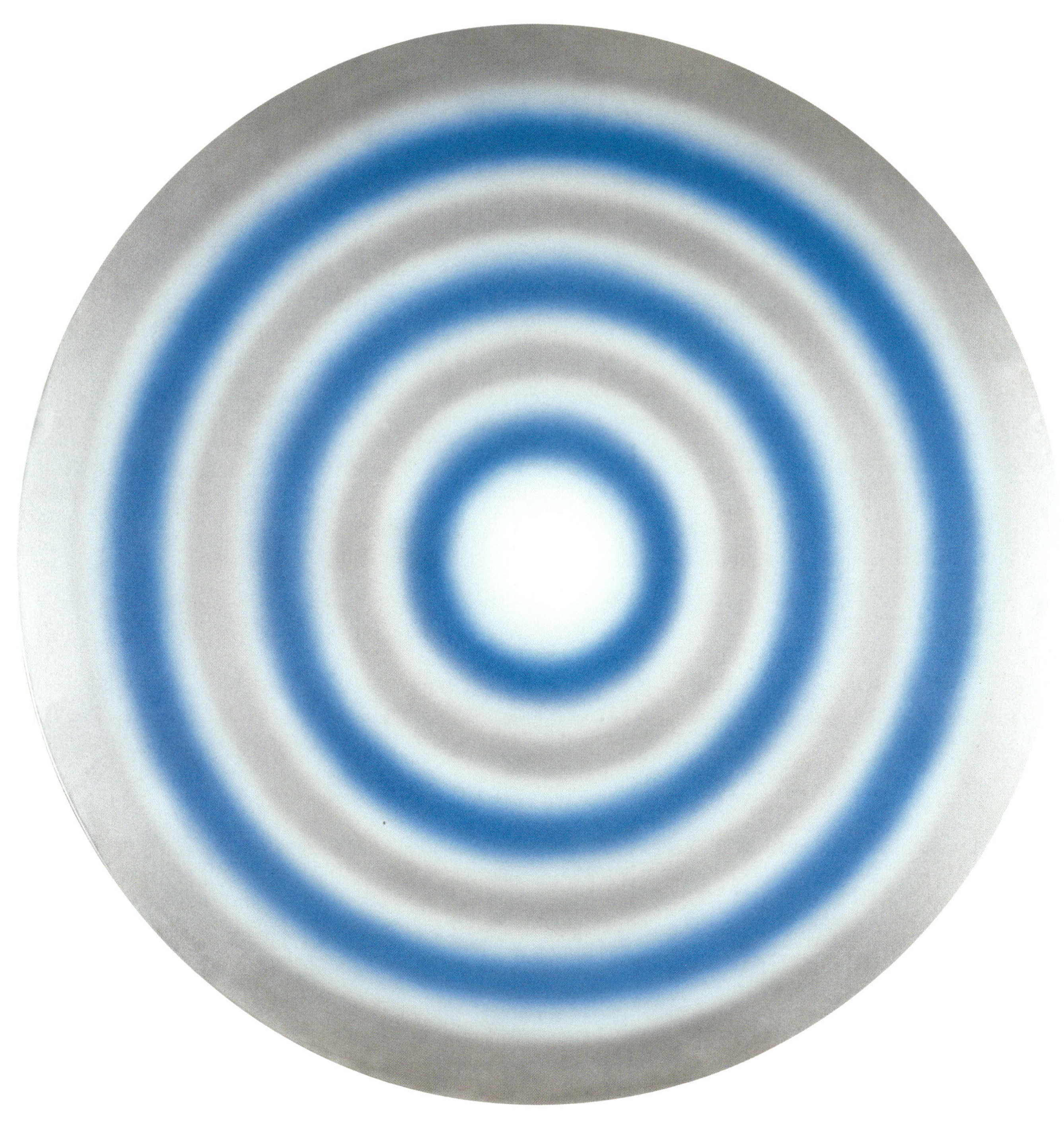

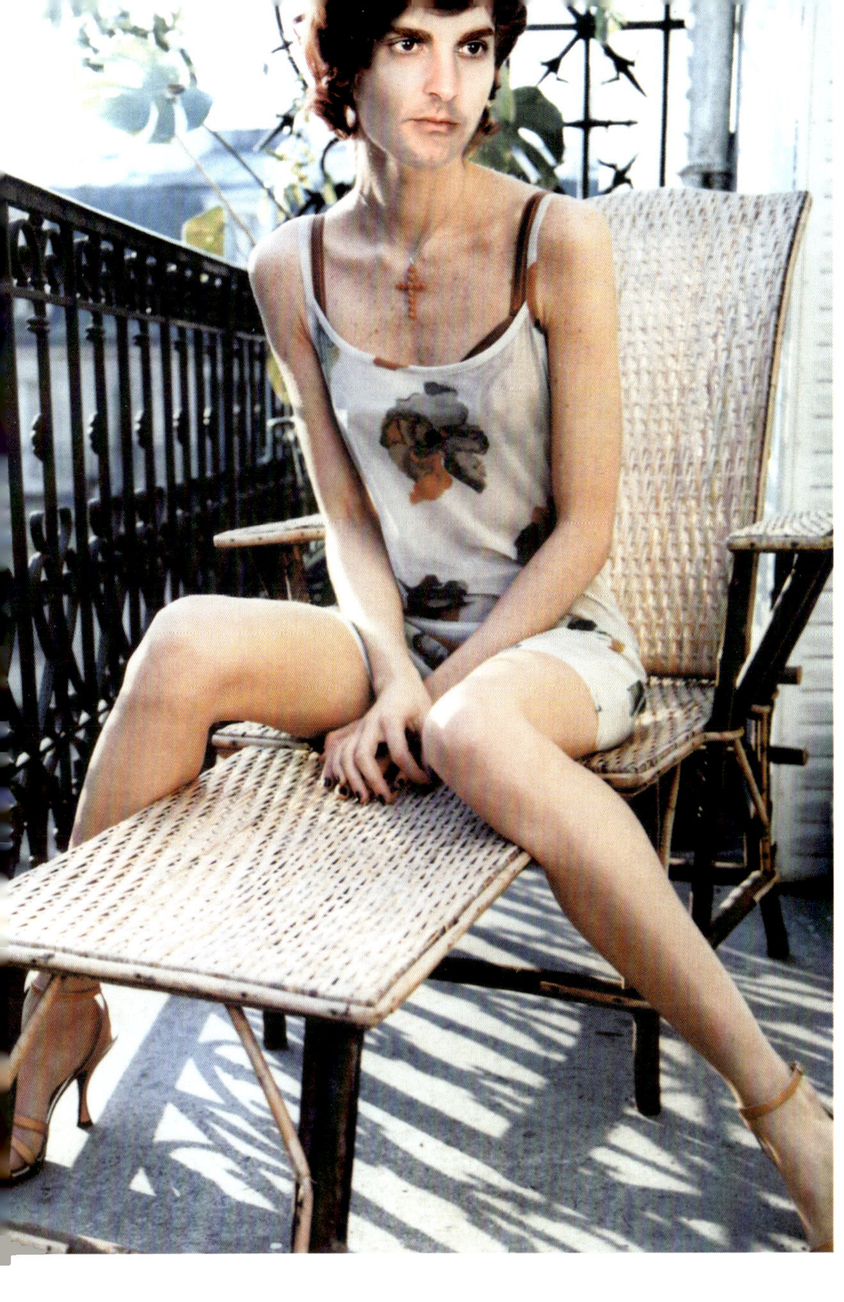
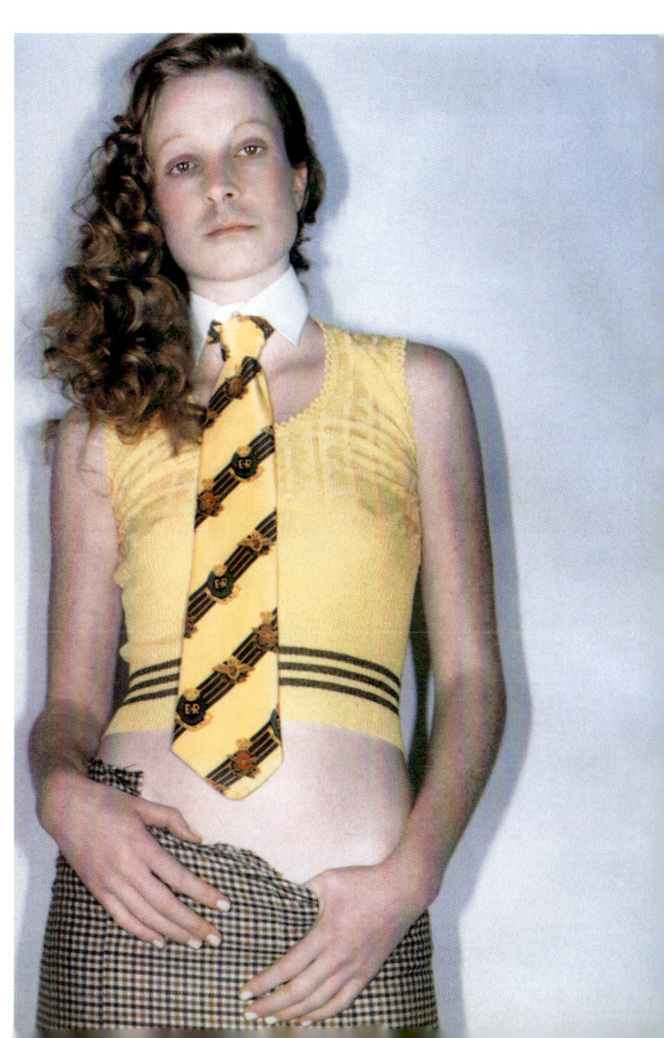

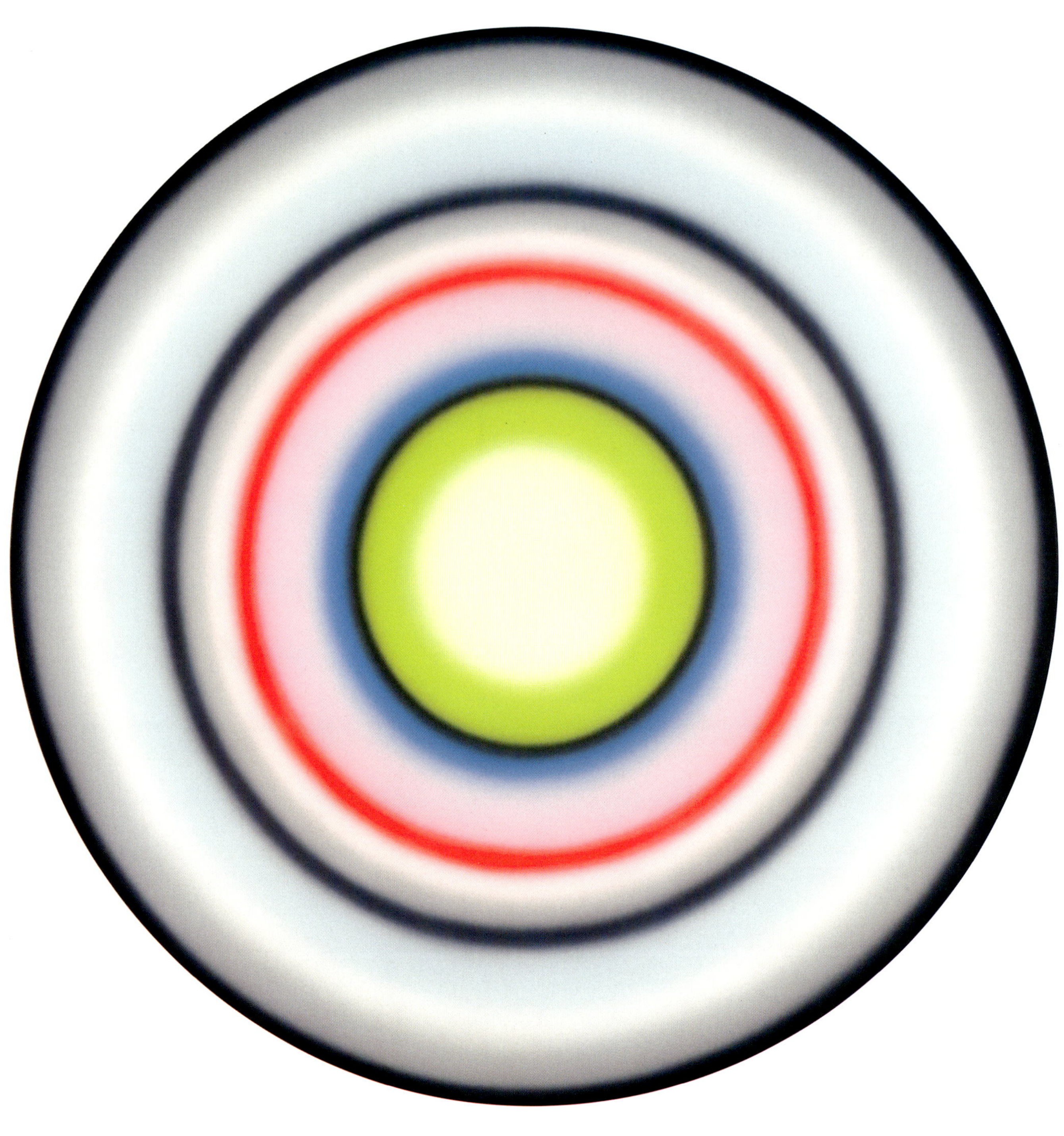

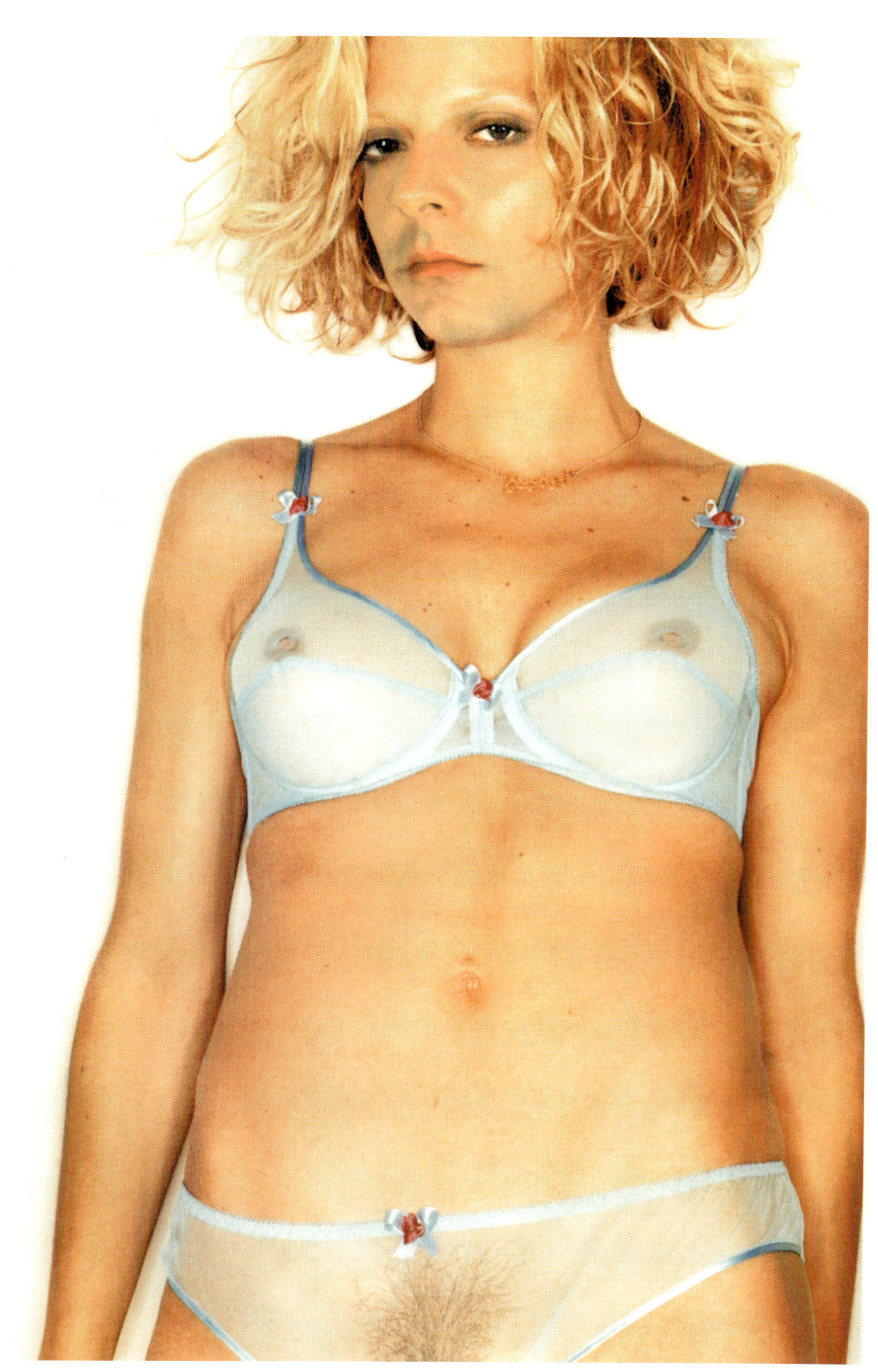

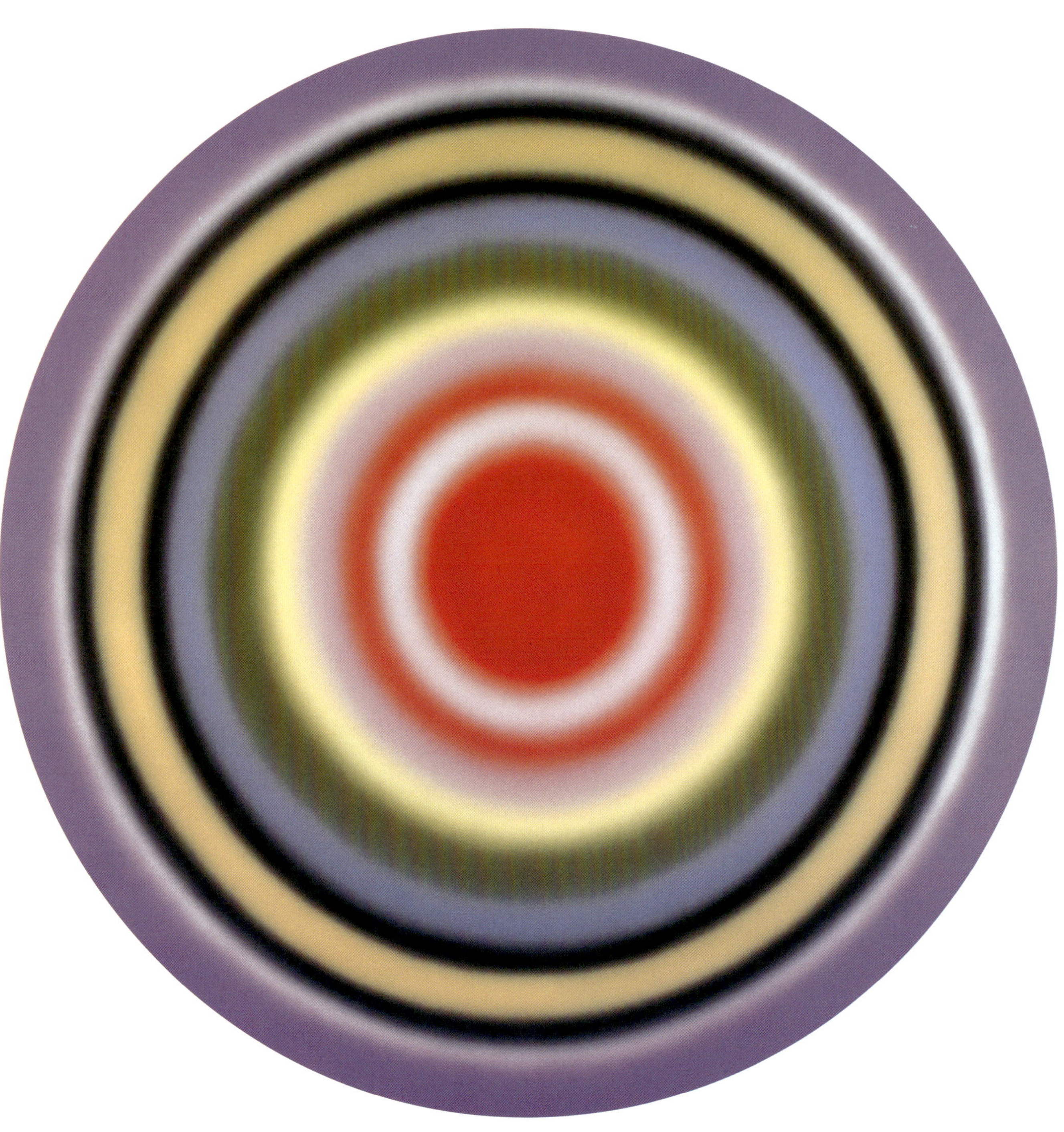

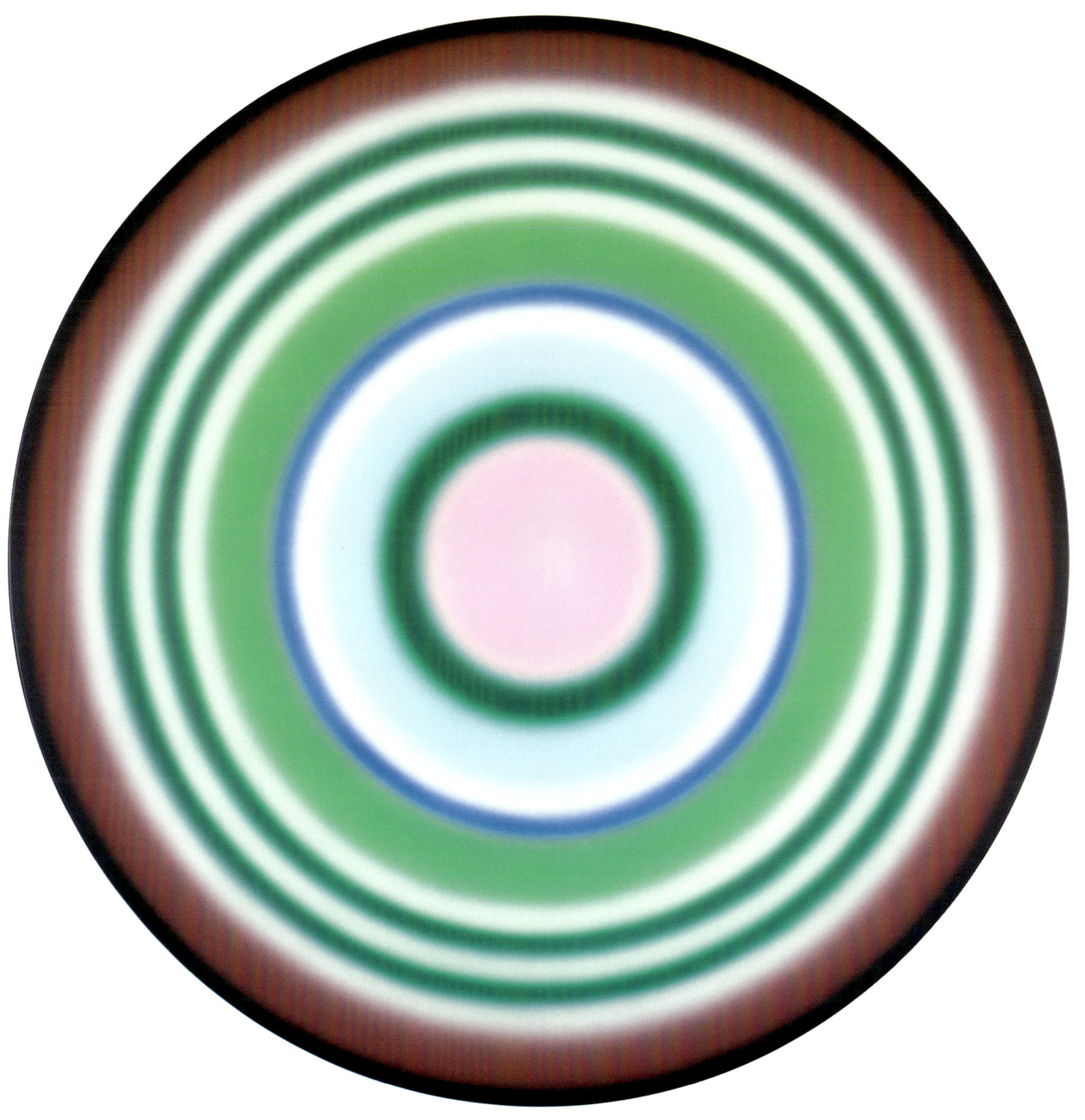

juan **uslé**

Mal de Sol 1994 112 x 198 cm

Yonker's Imperator 1995-96 274 x 203 cm

Welcome to the Eye 1994 203 x 274 cm

Soñé que Revelabas (Vanishing Lines) 1997 274 x 203 cm

Lineas de Madras 1995-97 178 x 203 cm

Rizoma's 1997 112 x 198 cm

Historia con Tres Nudos 1997 274 x 203 cm

mixed media on canvas

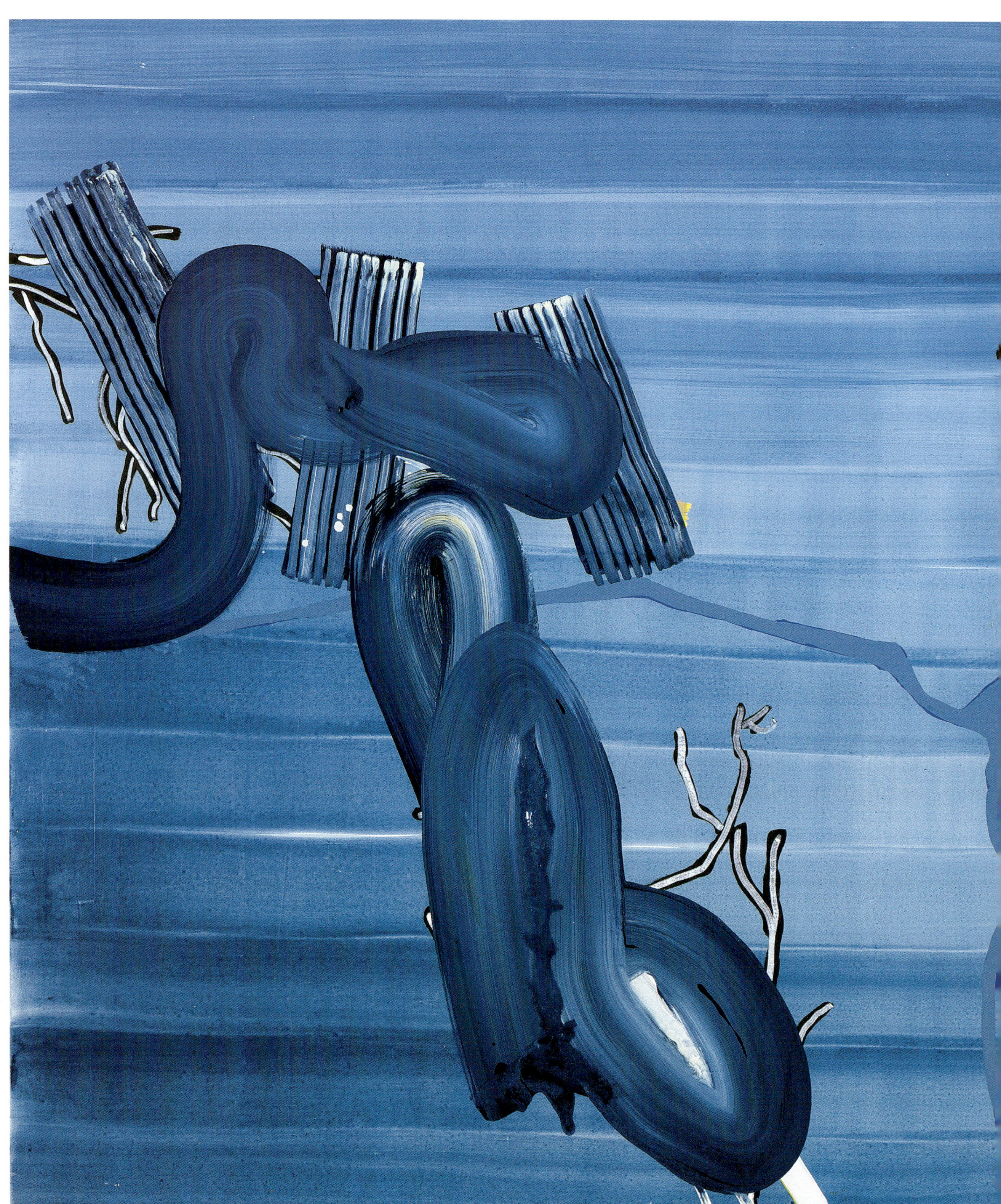

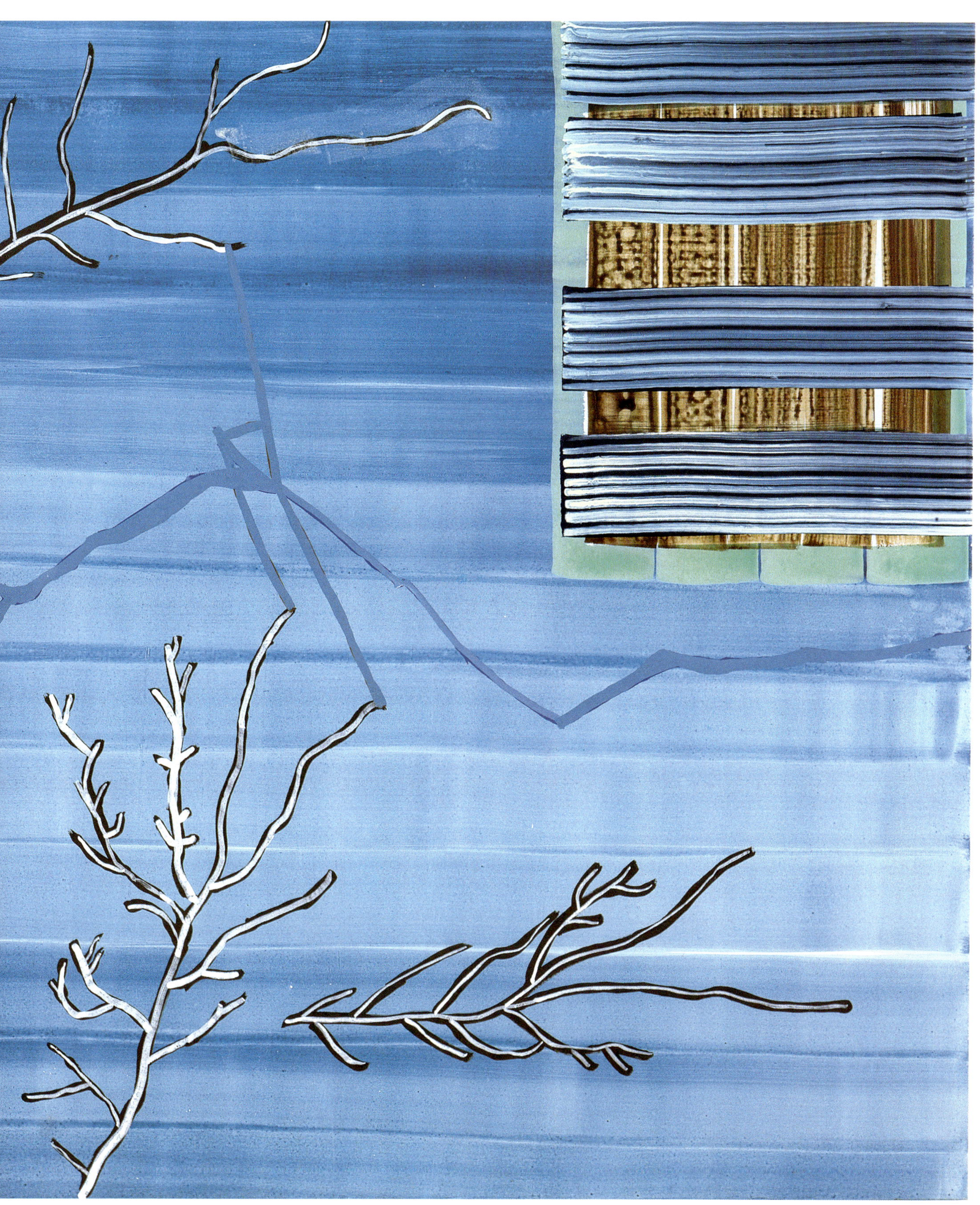

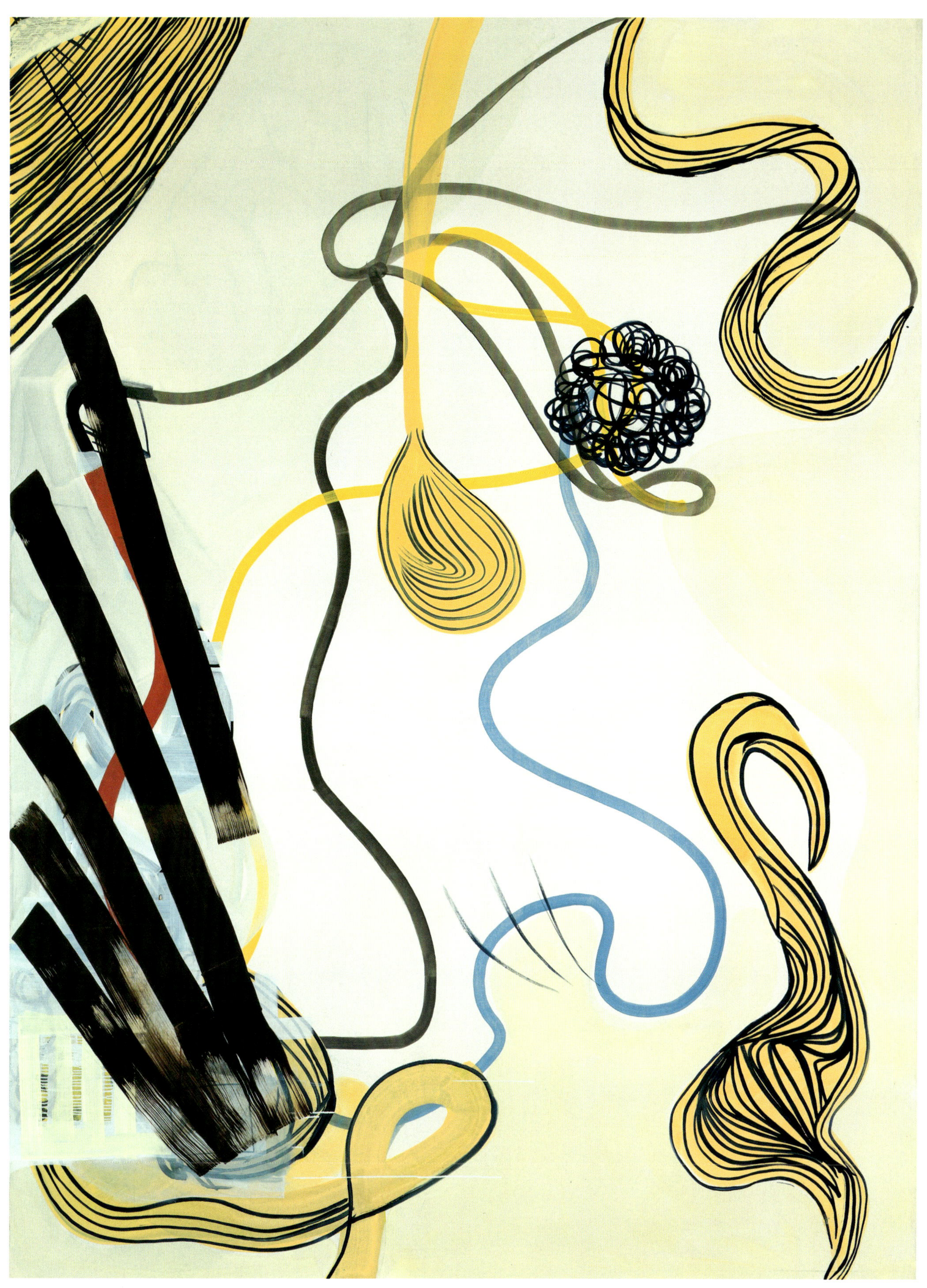

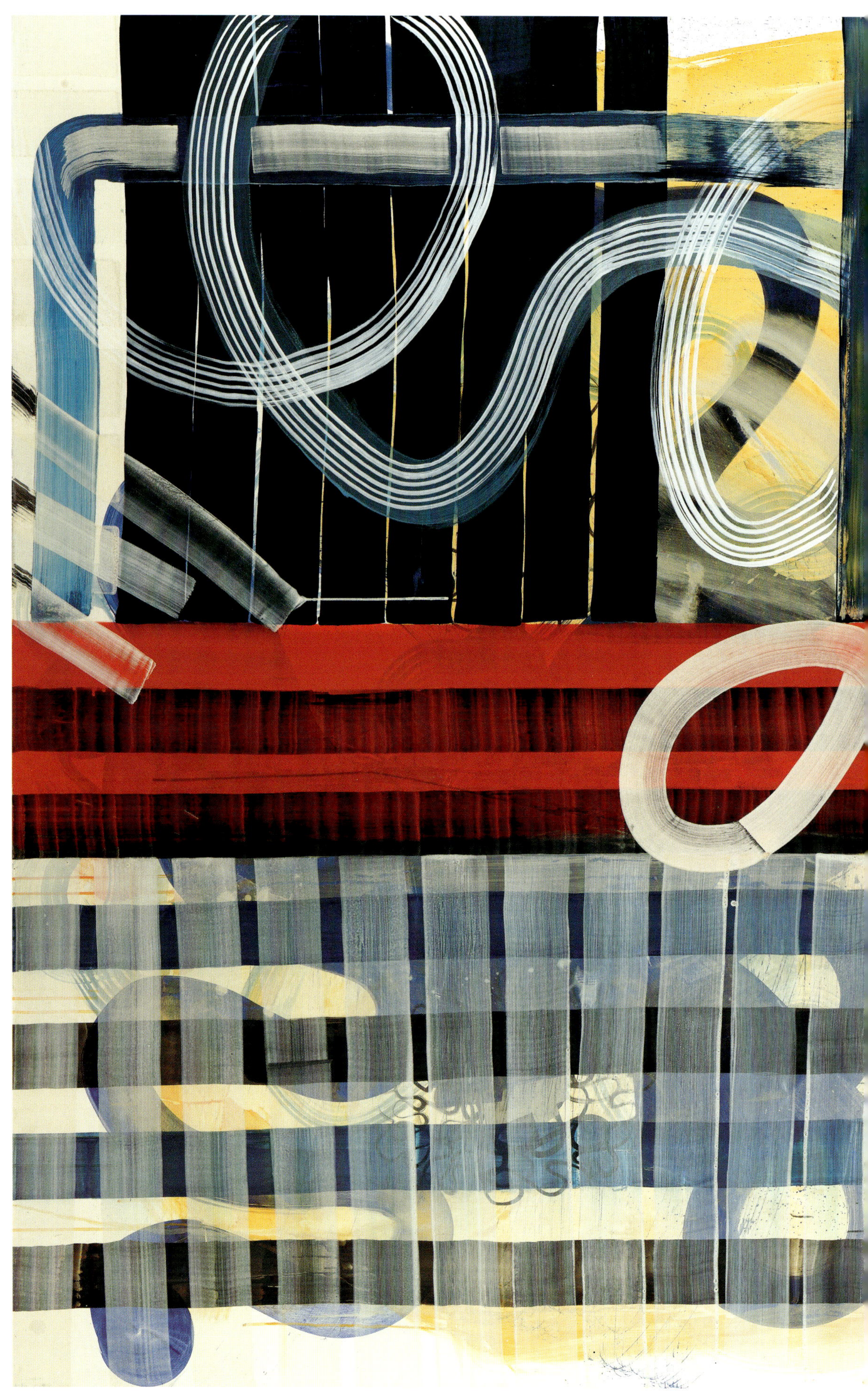

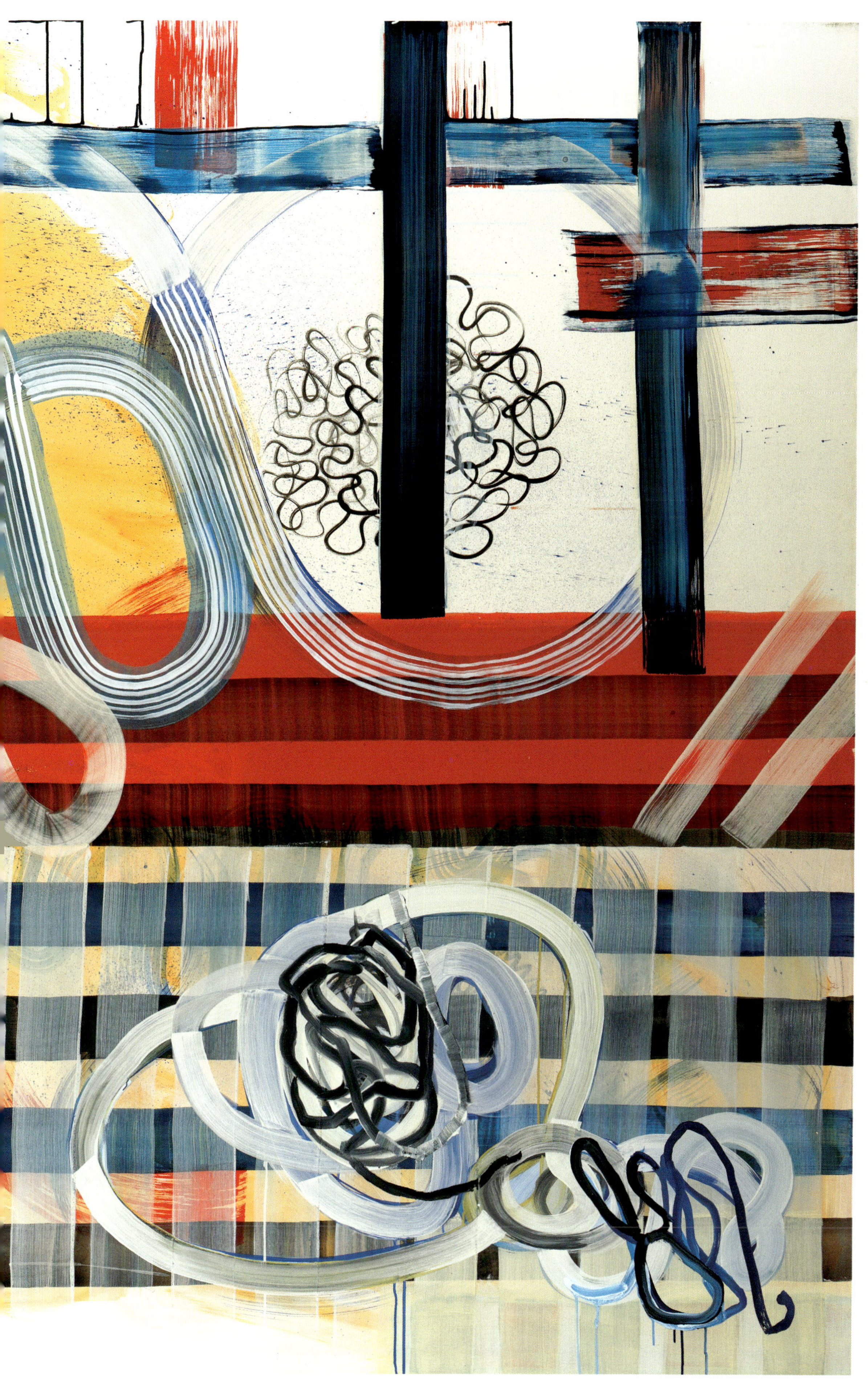

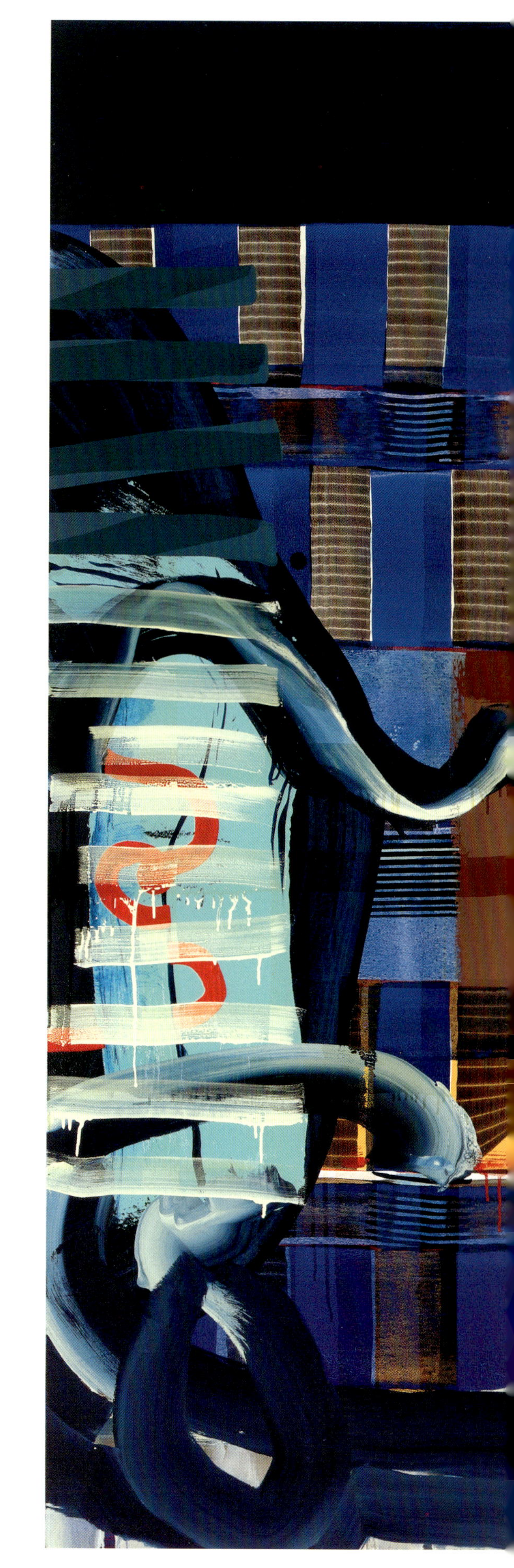

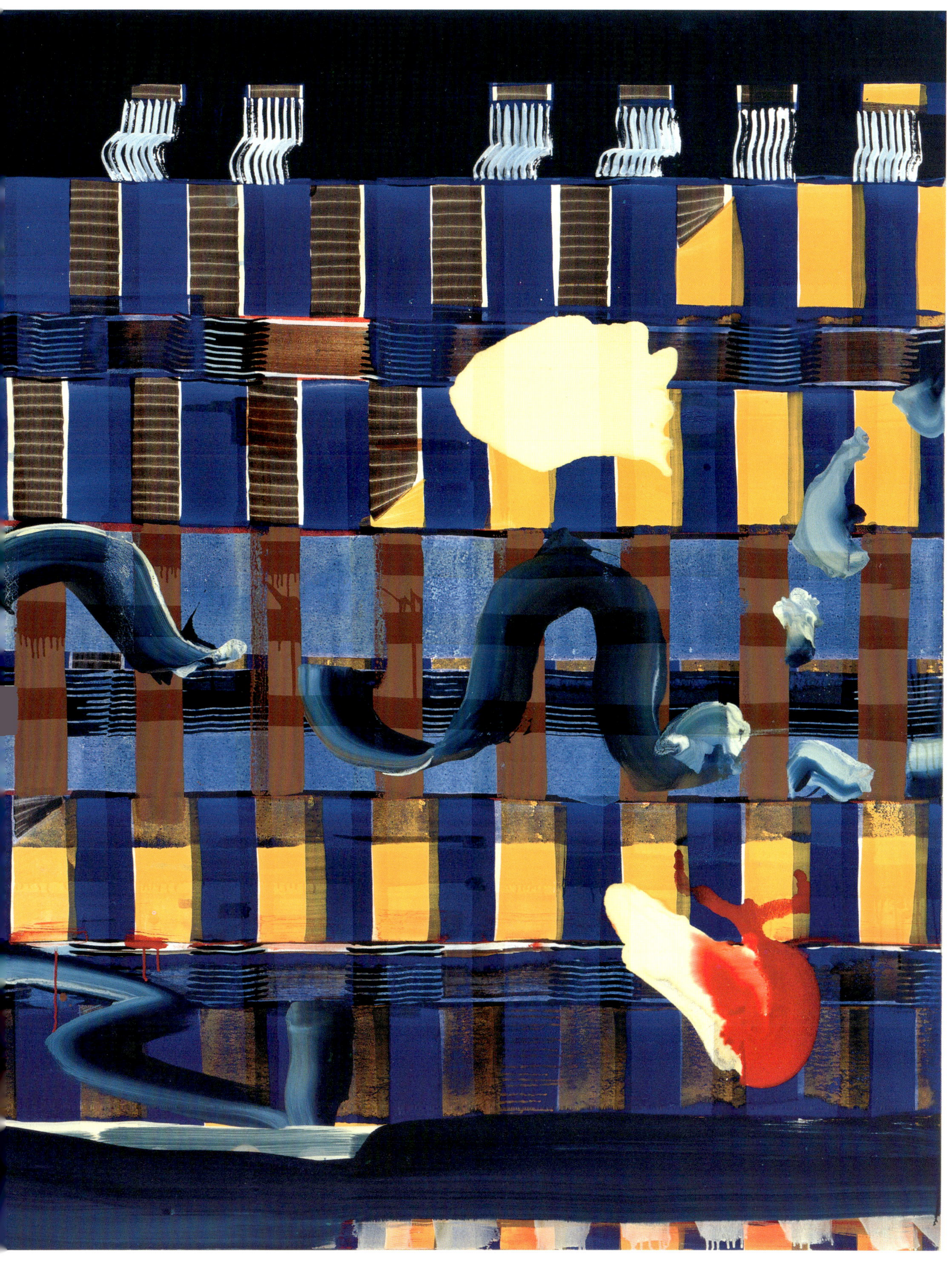

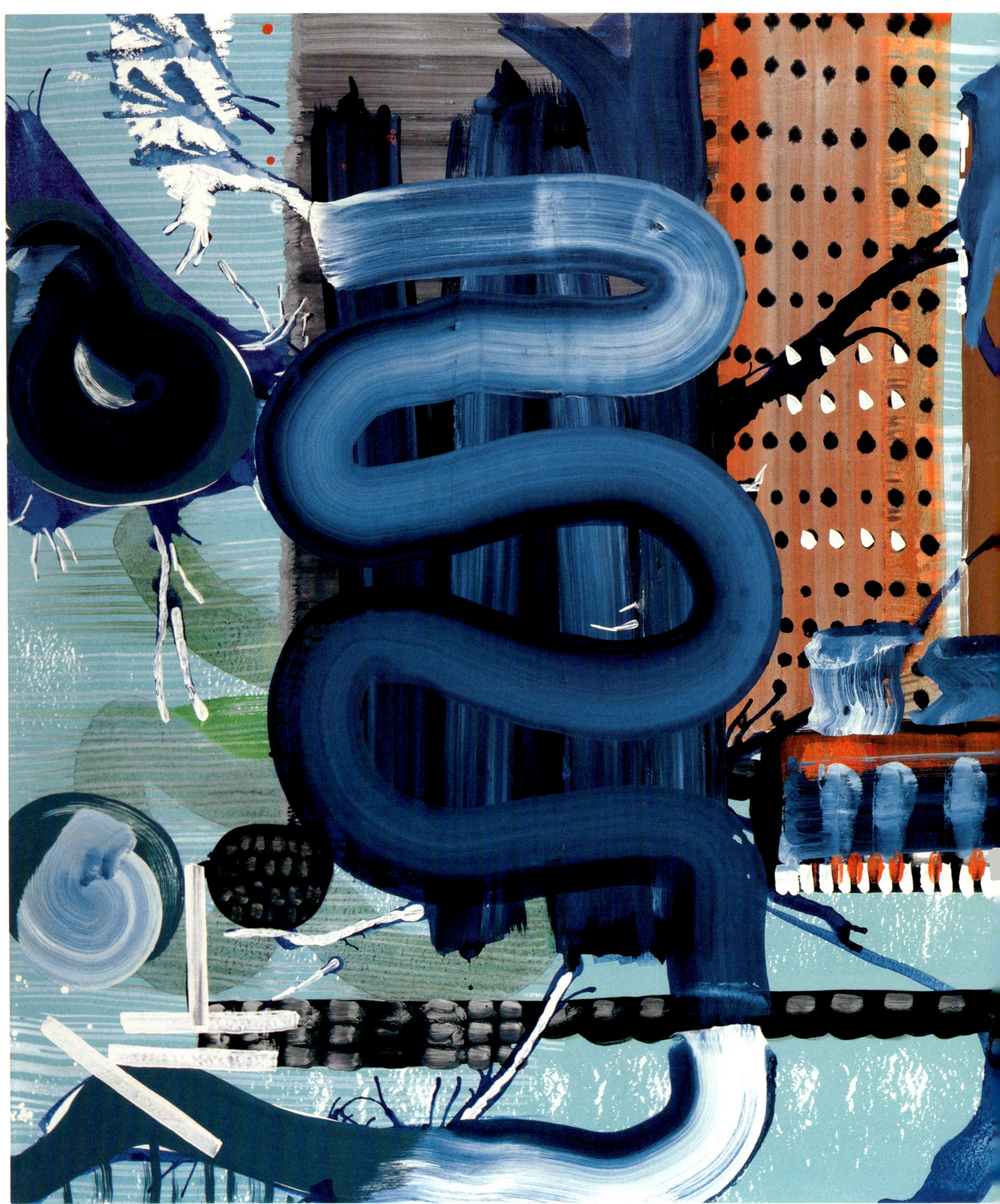

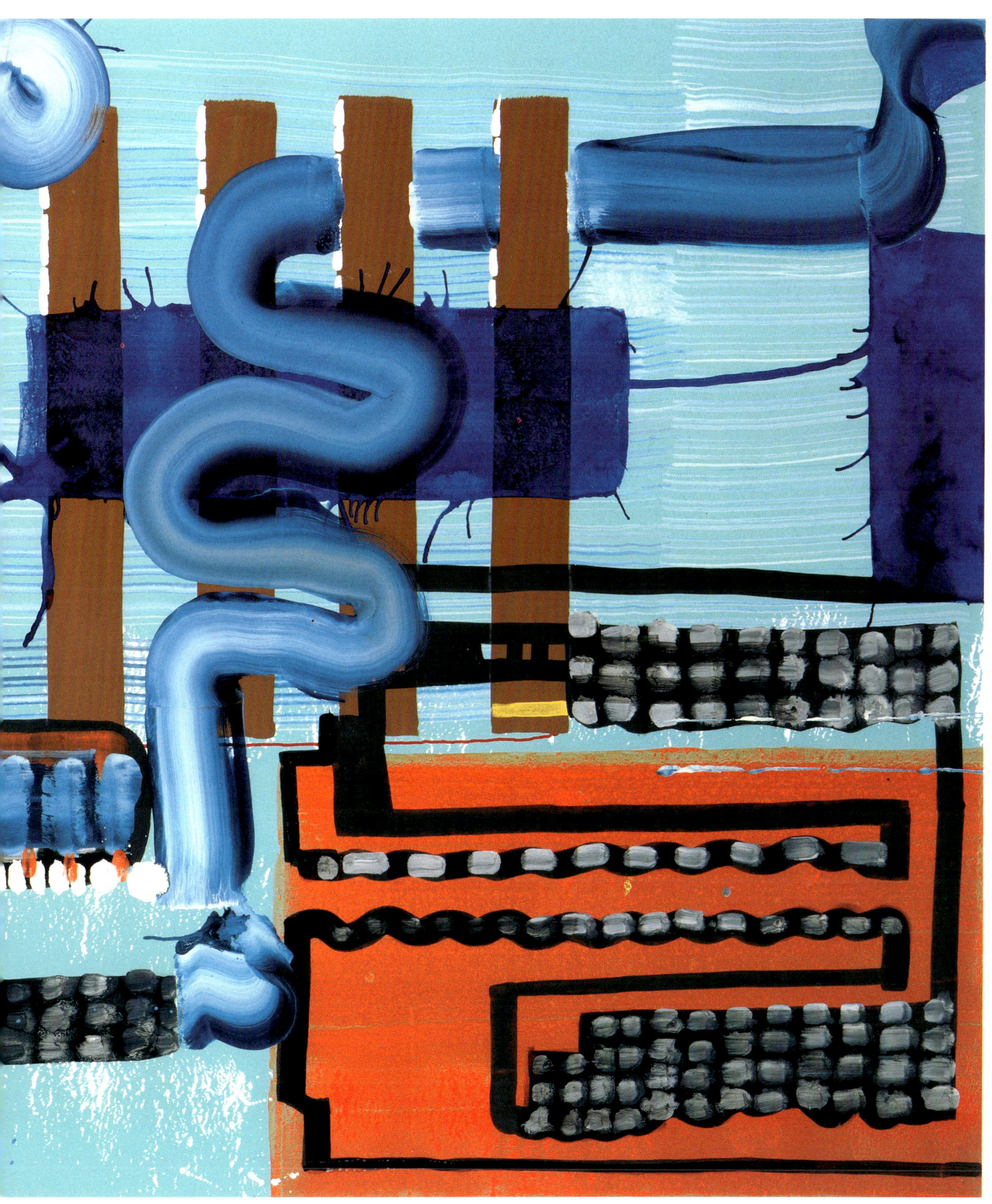

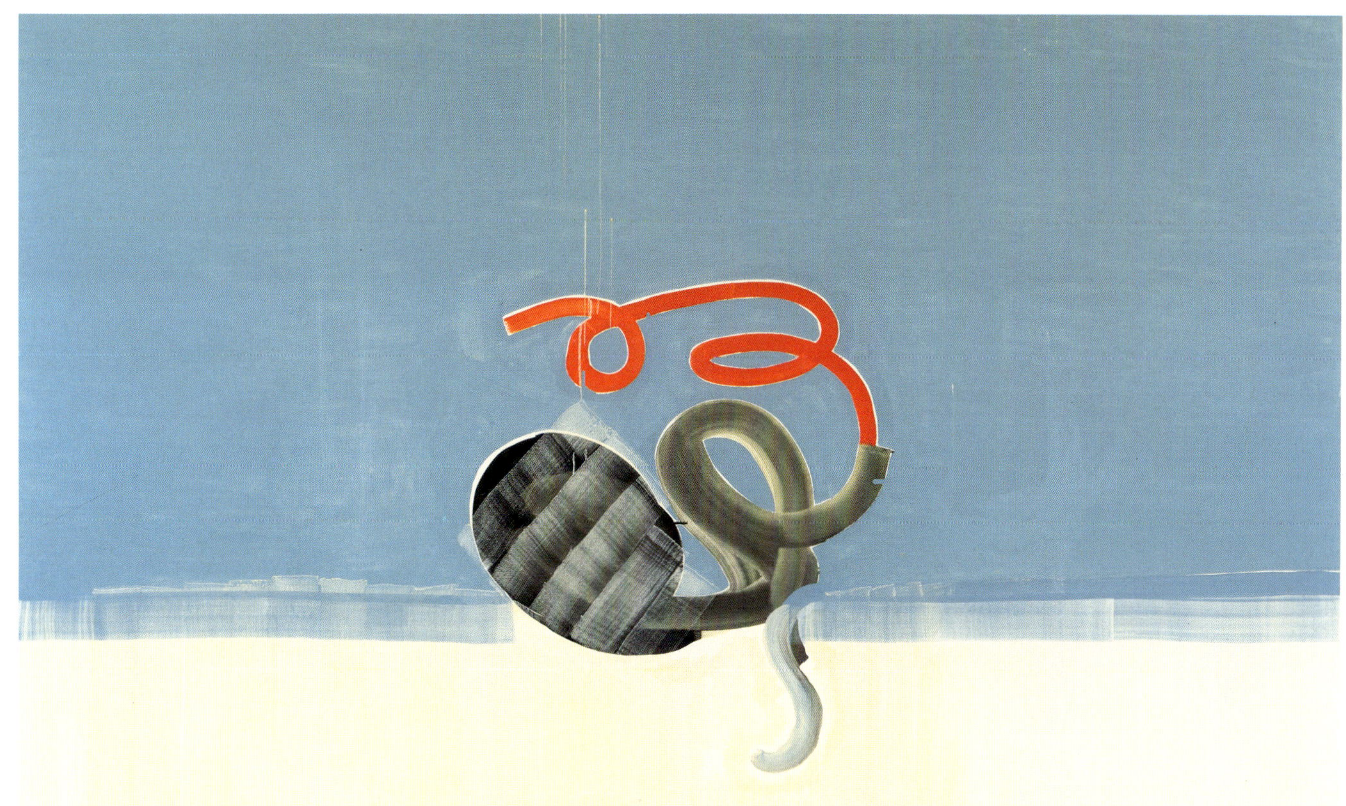
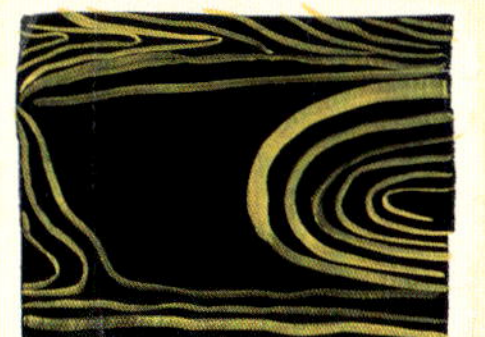

biographies

Thomas Demand

| 1964 | Born Munich, Germany |

EDUCATION

1987-89	Akademie der bildenden Künste, Munich
1989-92	Kunstakademie Düsseldorf
1992	Cité des Arts, Paris
1993-94	Goldsmiths' College, London (MA Fine Arts)
1995	Rijksakademie Amsterdam

Lives and works in Berlin

SOLO EXHIBITIONS

1991	Galerie Guy Ledune, Brussels
1992	Galerie Tanit, Munich
	Förderkoje Art Cologne
1994	Galerie Tanit, Munich
	Galerie Blancpain-Stepcynski, Geneva
1995	Victoria Miro Gallery, London
	Galerie Guy Ledune, Brussels
1996	Galerie de l'ancienne Poste, Le Channel, Calais
	Galerie Tanit, Munich
	Max Protetch Gallery, New York
1997	Monika Sprüth Gallery, Cologne
	Centre d'art contemporain de Vassivière en Limousin, Limousin
	Victoria Miro Gallery, London
1998	303 Gallery, New York
	Schipper & Krome, Berlin
	Kunstverein, Freiburg
	Kunsthalle, Bielefeld
	Galleria Monica de Cardenas, Milan
	Kunsthalle, Zürich

Rineke Dijkstra

1959   Born Sittard, Netherlands

EDUCATION
1981-86   Gerrit Rietveld Academie, Amsterdam

Lives and works in Amsterdam

SOLO EXHIBITIONS
1984	*Paradiso Portraits*, de Moor, Amsterdam
1988	*The Creation of Form*, de Moor, Amsterdam
1994	*Art Encouragement Award Amstelveen*, Aemstelle, Amstelveen
1995	Stedelijk Museum Bureau Amsterdam (with Tom Claassen)
	Time Festival, Rineke Dijkstra, Museum of Contemporary Art, Gent, Belgium (with Hugo Delbaere)
1996	Le Consortium, Dijon
	Galerie Sabine Schmidt, Cologne
	Galerie Bob van Orsouw, Zurich
	Galerie Paul Andriesse, Amsterdam
1997	Galerie Mot & Van den Boogaard, Belgium
	The Photographers' Gallery, London
1998	Museum Folkwang, Essen
	Sprengel Museum, Hannover
	Boymans Van Beuningen, Rotterdam

Esko Männikkö

1959   Born in Pudasjärvi, Finland

Lives and works in Oulu

SOLO EXHIBITIONS
1982-83	*When Time Stops Still*, Rantagalleria Öulo, (tour Helsinki, Pudasjärvi)
1989	*Irylli*, Öulo, Utajärvi
1990-91	*Sitä pittää ihmisen olla viisas*, Ylivieska, Sodankylä
1992-93	*Kotikäynti*, Öulo, Joensuu
1992	*Home Visit*, Rantagalleria, Öulo
1993	*Naarashauki*, Helsinki
1993-94	*Pemoht*, photographs of the environmental destruction of the Kola Peninsula (together with Pekka Turunen), St. Petersburg, Pietan, Murmansk, Apatiitti, Kirovsk, Oulo
	Female Pike, Hippolyte Photo Gallery, Helsinki
1995	*Young Artist of the Year 1995*, Tampere Art Museum, Tampere
	Morris Healy Gallery, New York
	Galerie Nordenhake, Stockholm
1996-97	Portikus, Frankfurt am Main (cat.)
	DE PONT, Tilburg (cat.)
	Lenbachhaus, Munich (cat.)
	Société des Expositions du Palais des Beaux-Arts, Brussels (cat.)
	Mexas, Art Pace, San Antonio
1997-98	Malmö Konsthall, Malmö
	Hippolyte Photo Gallery, Helsinki
	Thomas Healy Gallery, New York

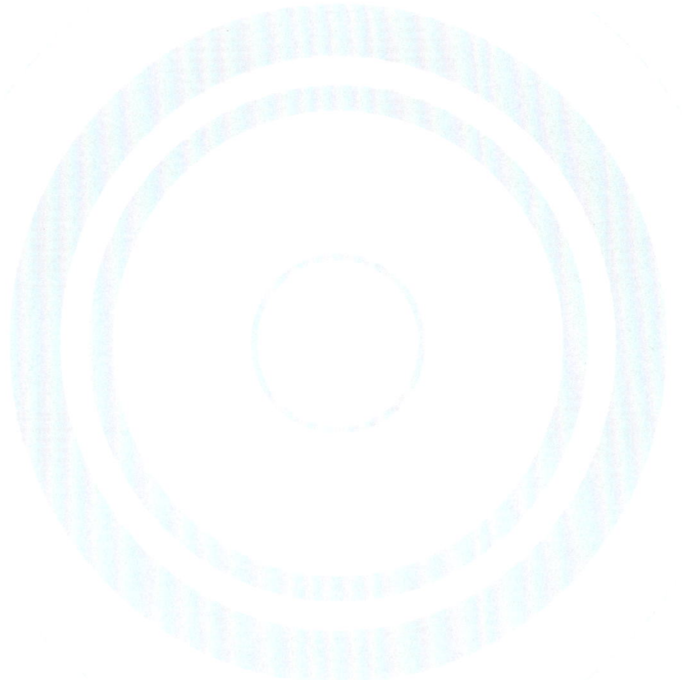

Ugo Rondinone

1963   Born Brunnen, Switzerland

EDUCATION
1986-90   Hochschule für angewandte Kunst, Vienna

Lives and works in Zurich and New York

SOLO EXHIBITIONS
1985   Galerie Marlene Frei, Zurich
1986   sec52, Ricco Bilger, Zurich
1987   Raum für aktuelle Schweizer Kunst, Luzern
1989   Galerie Pinx, Oskar Schmidt, Vienna
1990   Kunstmuseum Luzern, Luzern - Ausstellungspreis (cat.)
1991   Galerie Walcheturm, Zurich
      Galerie Pinx, Oskar Schmidt, Vienna
      Galerie Martina Detterer, Franfurt am Main
1992   Galerie Walcheturm, Zurich
1993   Galerie Ballgasse (Pakesch & Stejskal), Vienna
      Centre d'Art Contemporain de Martigny, Martigny
1994   Galerie Six Friedrich, Munich
      Galerie Daniel Buchholz, Cologne
1995   Galerie Walcheturm, Zurich
      Migrateurs, ARC Museé d'Art Moderne de la Ville de Paris, Paris (cat.)
      Galerie Froment - Putman, Paris
1996   *heyday*, Centre d'Art Contemporain, Geneva (cat.)
      Dog days are over, Museum für Gegenwartskunst, Zurich (cat.)
      Le Case d'Arte, Milan
      Where do we go from here?, Biennale Sao Paulo (cat.)
1997   *Moonlight and Aspirin*, Galleria Bonomo, Rome
      Still Smoking, Galleria Raucci/St. Maria, Naples
      Where do we go from here?, Le Consortium, Dijon
      tender places come from nothing, Cato Jans Der Raum, Hamburg
1998   Galerie Almine Rech, Paris
      Galerie Joao Graca 1990, Lisbon
      So much water, so close to home, Krobath & Wimmer, Vienna
1999   Galerie für Zeitgenössische Kunst Leipzig, Leipzig
      Kunsthaus Glarus, Glarus (cat.)
      Schipper & Krome, Berlin

Juan Uslé

1954	Born in Santander, Spain

EDUCATION/WORK EXPERIENCE

1973-77	Belas Artes, Escuela Superior of San Carlos, Valencia
1978-79	Works in collaboration with Victoria Civera, alternative photographer, photomontage and painting
1980	Receives grant from Minister of Culture for "Contexto"
1982	Receives grant from Minister of Culture for "Nuevas Formas Expresivas"
1984	Professor for the University of Cantabria
1986	Receives grant from the Spanish-American joint committee for cultural exchange

Lives and works in Saro (Cantabria) and New York

SOLO EXHIBITIONS

1977	Galería Pombera, Noja
1978	Galería Val I Trenta, Valencia
	C.E.M. de Sipe, Valencia
1979	Galería Puntal 2, Torrelavega
	Galería Joaquin Mir, Palma de Mallorca
1980	Galería II, Alicante
1981	Museo Municipal de Bellas Artes de Santander
	Galería Ruiz Castillo, Madrid
	Galería Lloc d'Art Elx
1982	Galería Palau, Valencia
1983	Galería Montenegro, Madrid
1984	Galería Ciento, Barcelona
	Fundación Botín, Santander
	Galería Nicanor Piñole, Gijón
1985	*Currents*, Institute of Contemporary Art, Boston, MA,
	Galería Montenegro, Madrid
	Galería Windsor Kulturgintza, Bilbao
	Galerie 121, Antwerp
1986	Galería La Máquina Españole, Seville
	Palacete Embarcadero, Santander
1987	Galería Montenegro, Madrid
	Galerie Farideh Cadot, Paris
1988	Farideh Cadot Gallery, New York
	Galería Fernando Silió, Santander
1989	Galería Montenegro, Madrid
	Galerie Farideh Cadot, Paris
	Farideh Cadot Gallery, New York
1990	Galerie Barbara Farber, Amsterdam
1991	Galerie Farideh Cadot, Paris
	Galería Soledad Lorenzo, Madrid
	Palacete Embarcadero e Nave Sotoliva, Santander
1992	Galería Joan Prats, Barcelona
	Sala de Exposicións do Banco Zaragozano, Zaragoza
	John Good Gallery, New York
1993	Galería Soledad Lorenzo, Madrid
	Anders Tornberg Gallery, Lund, Sweden
	Galerie Barbara Farber, Amsterdam
1994	Frith Street Gallery, London
	Galerie Bob van Orsouw, Zürich
	Sala Amós Salvador, Logroño
	Feigen Gallery, Chicago
	XXIII Bienal de Potevedra
	John Good Gallery, New York
1995	*Juan Uslé Obra 1994-1995: mal de sol,* Galería Soledad Lorenzo, Madrid
	Juan Uslé, Galerie Daniel Templon, Paris
	Juan Uslé, Robert Miller Gallery, New York
	Galerie Buchmann, Cologne
1996	Museu d'art Contemporani de Barcelona, Spain, travelled to Kunsthalle Bielefeld, Germany
	Anders Tornberg Gallery, Lund, Sweden
	L.A. Louver Gallery, Los Angeles, CA
1996-97	IVAM, Centre del Carme, Spain, Curated by Kevin Powers

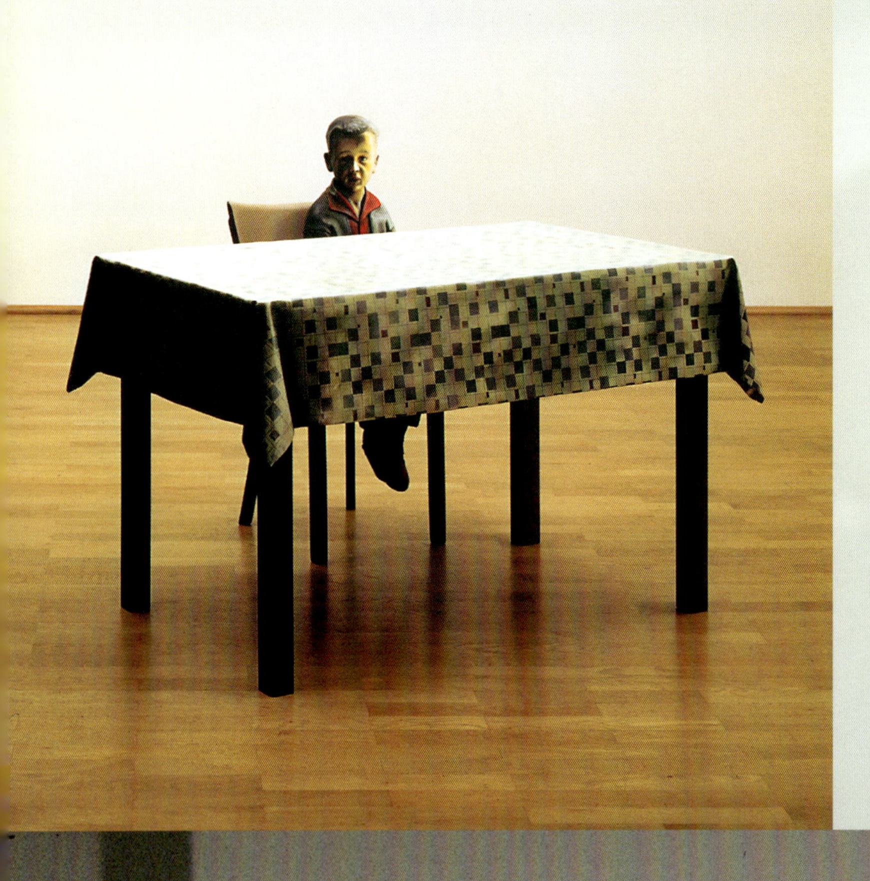
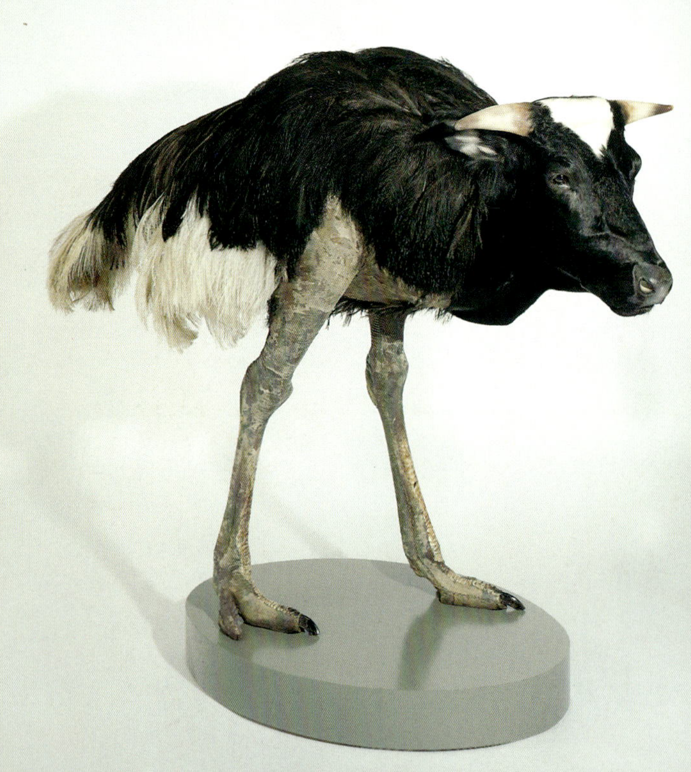

YOUNG GERMAN ARTISTS 2 AT THE SAATCHI GALLERY

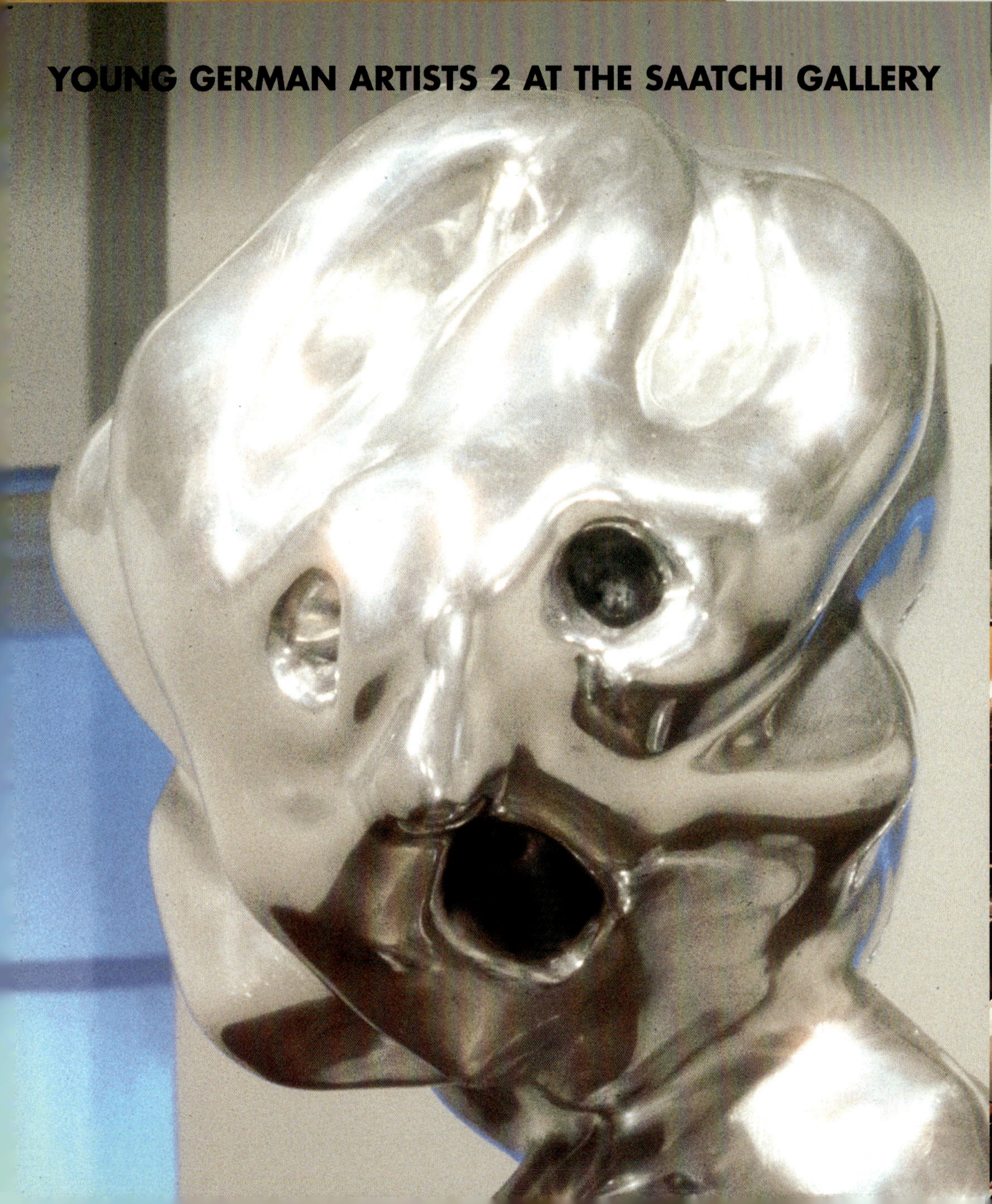

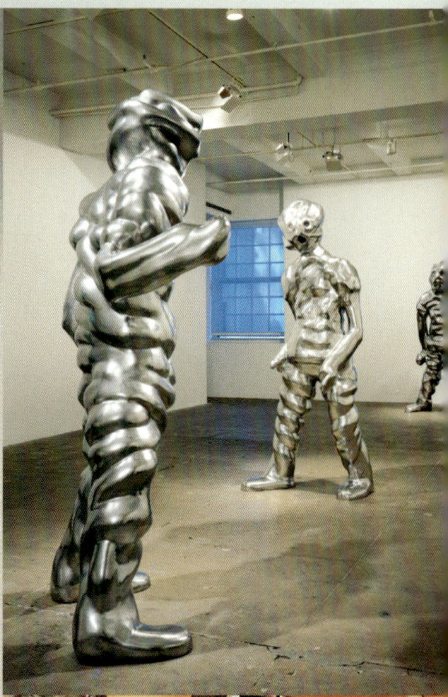

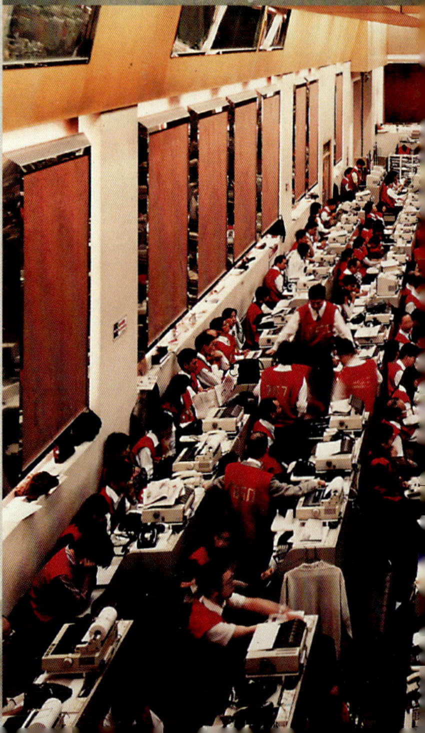

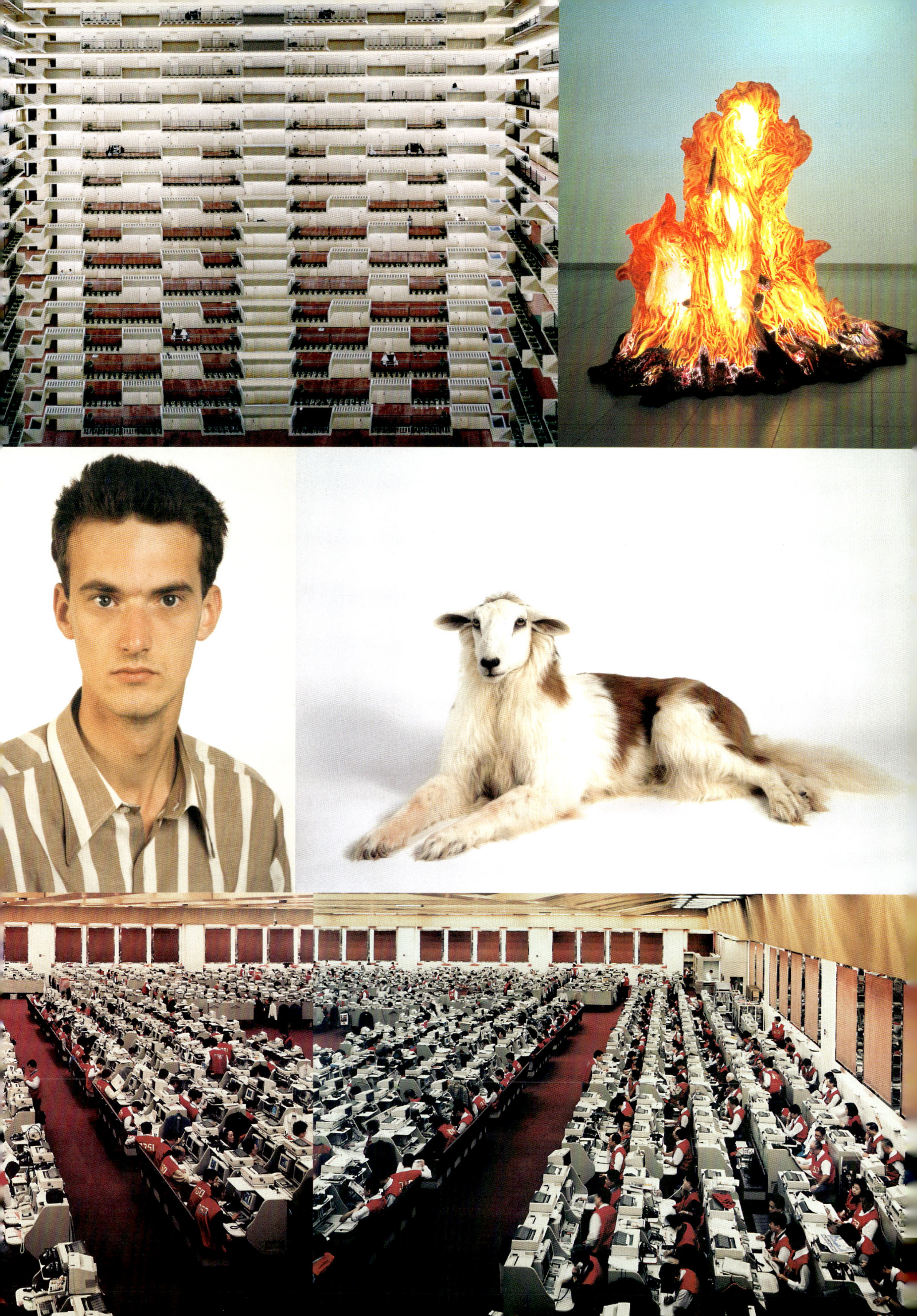

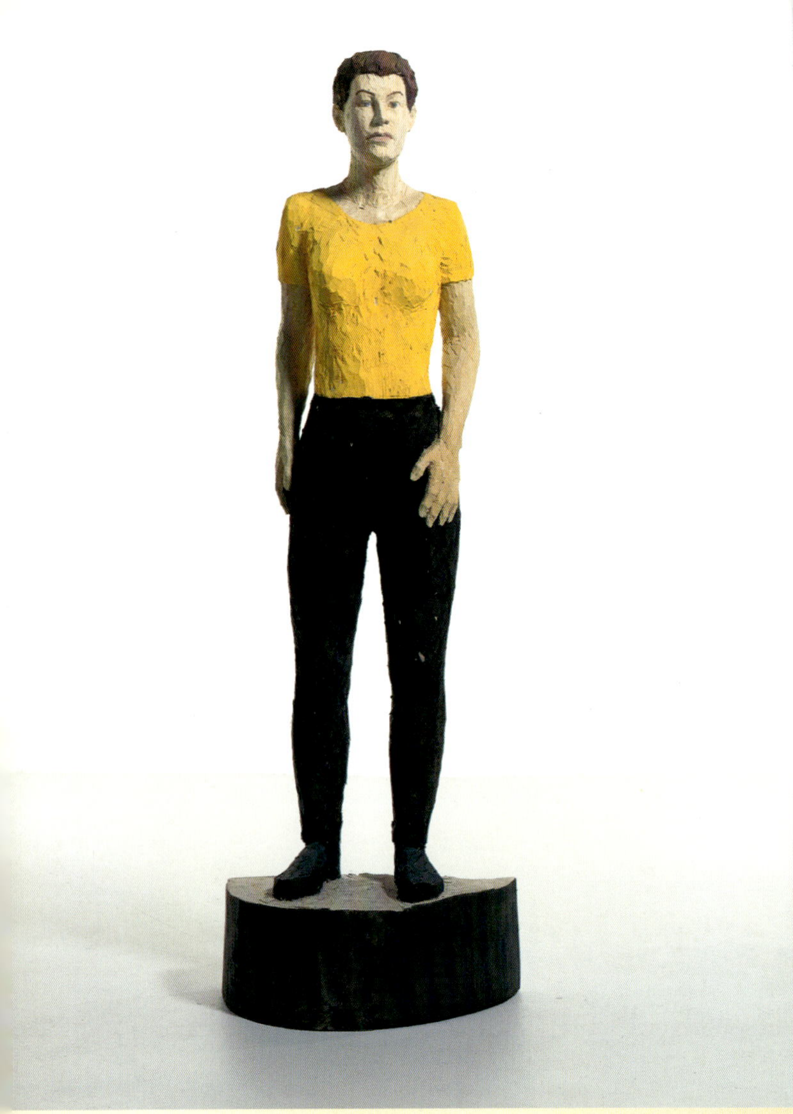

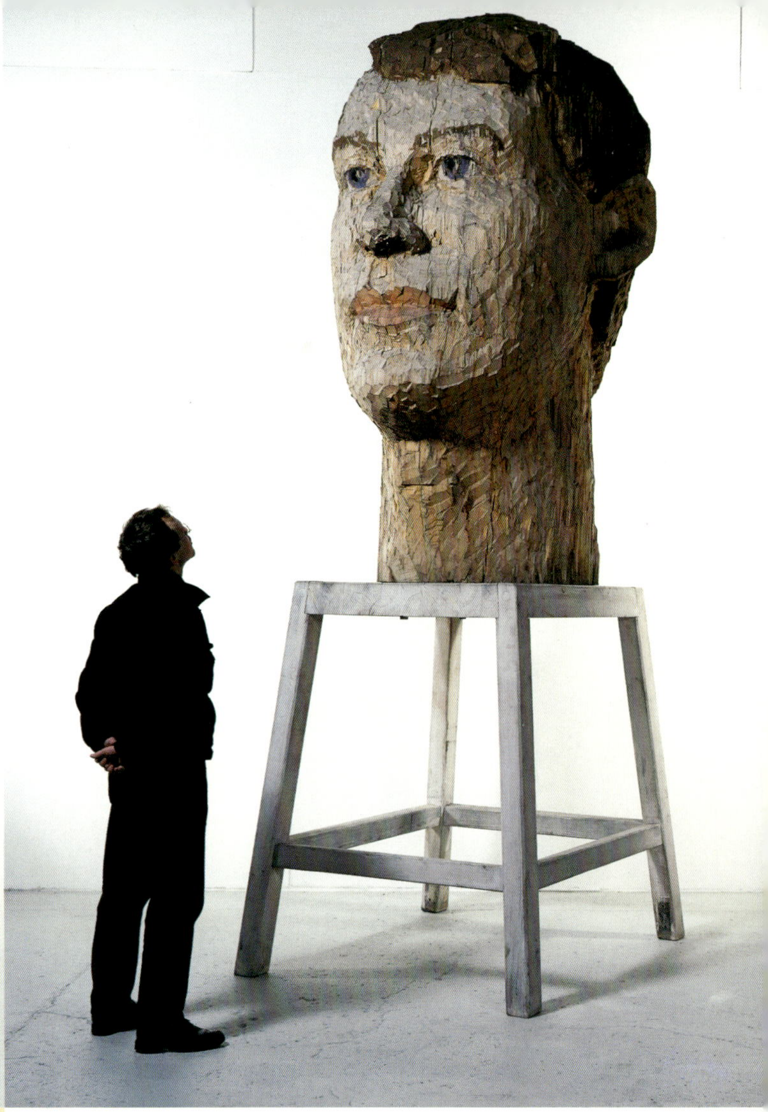

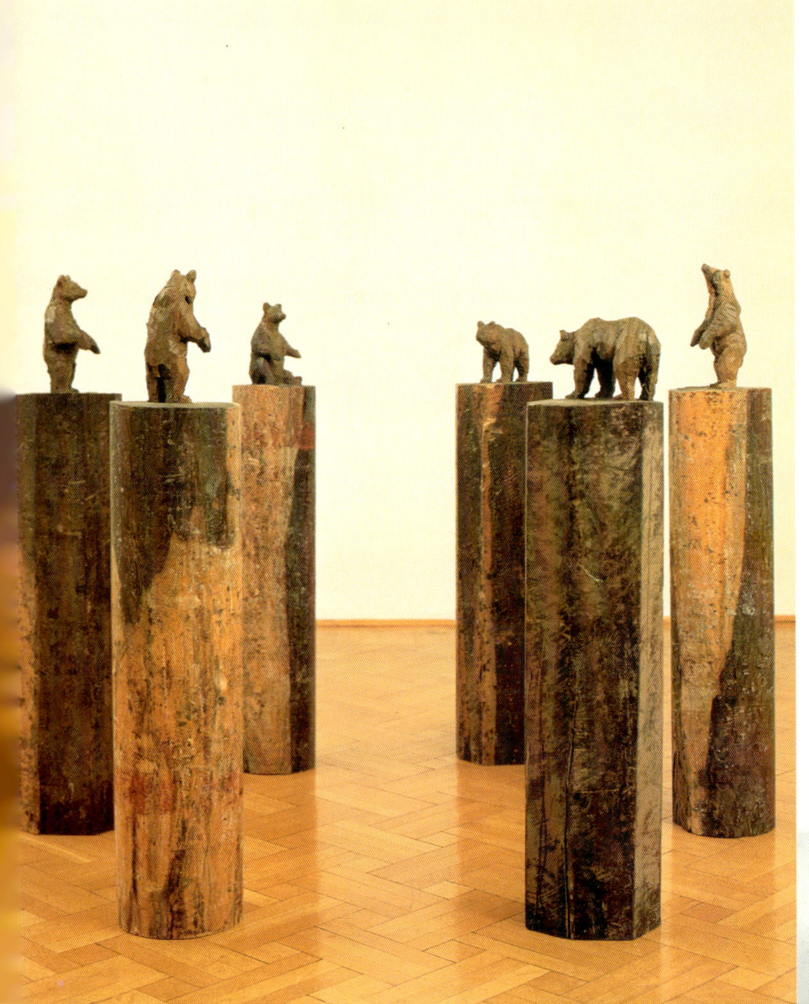
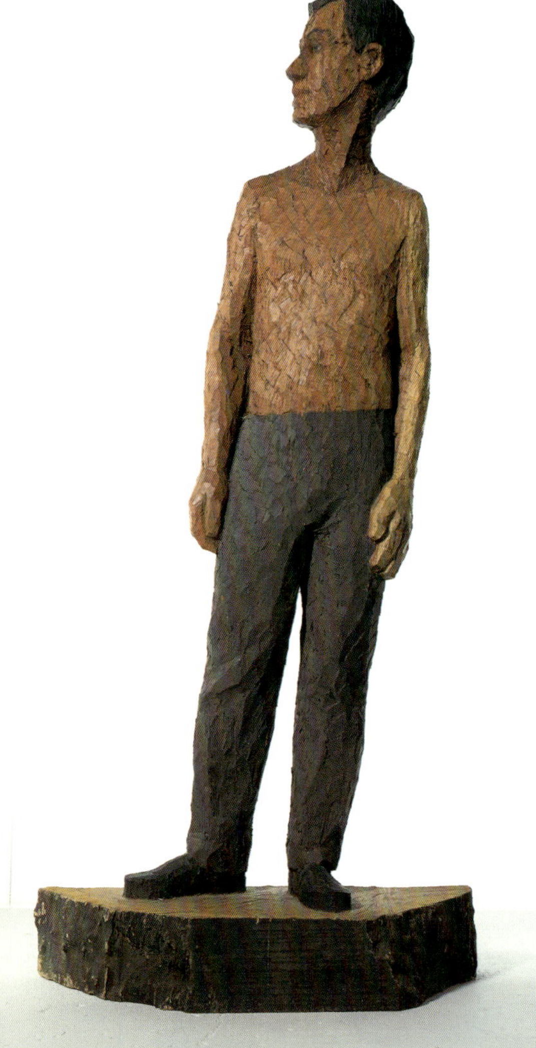

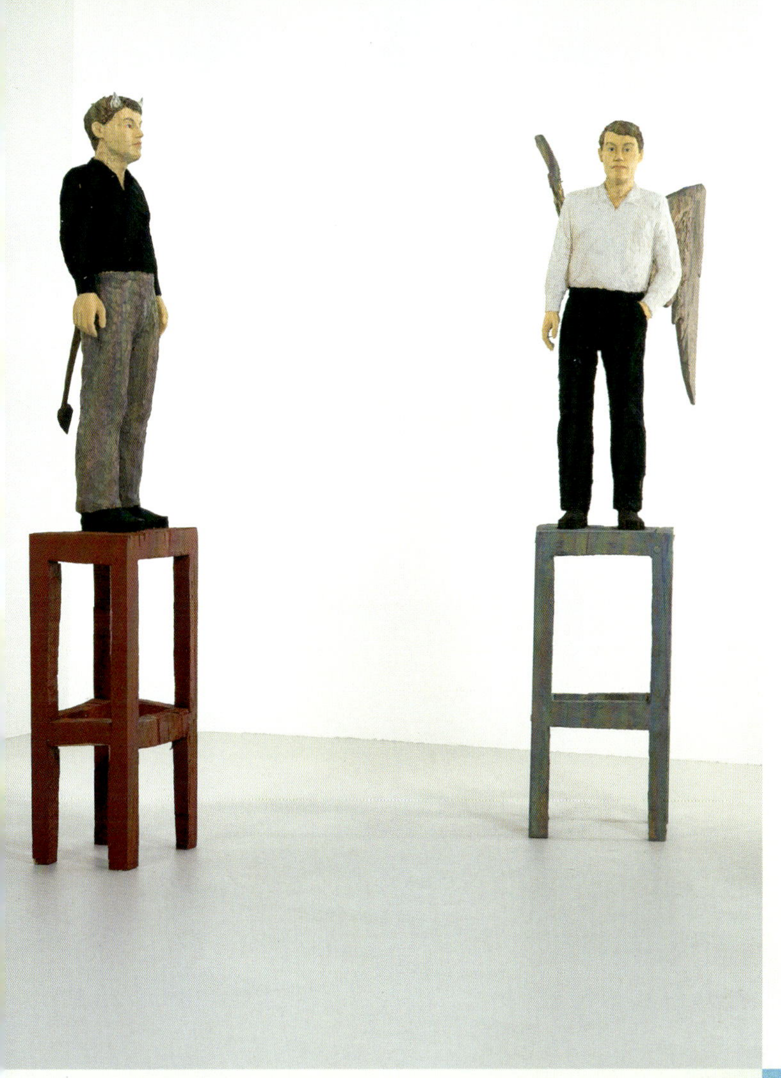

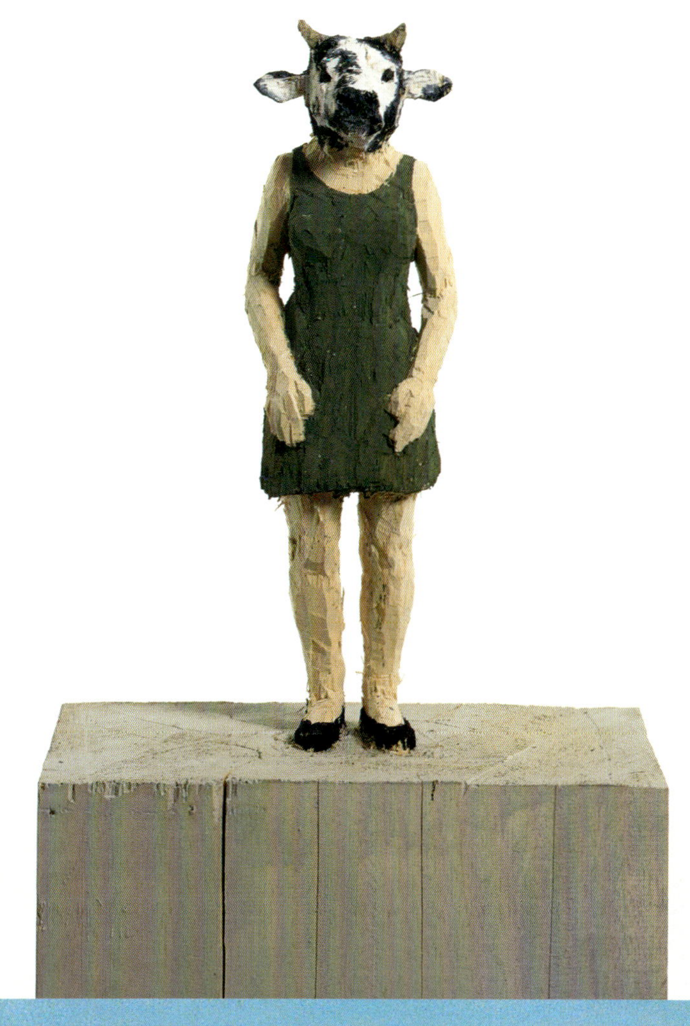

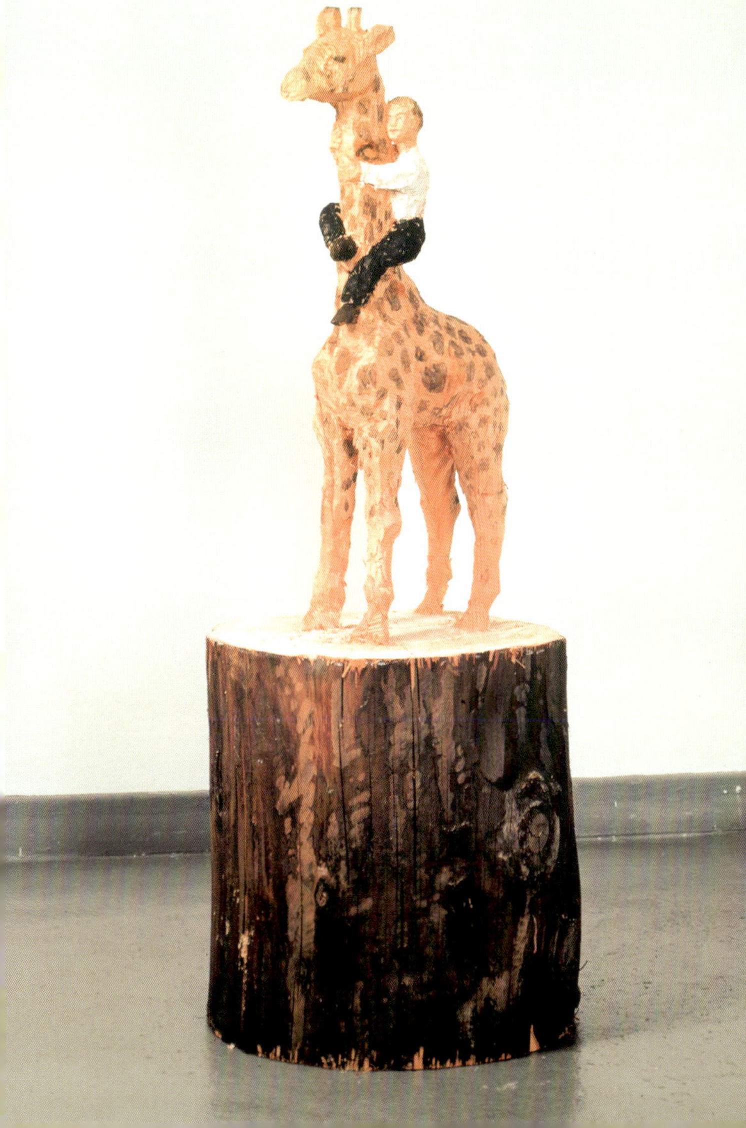

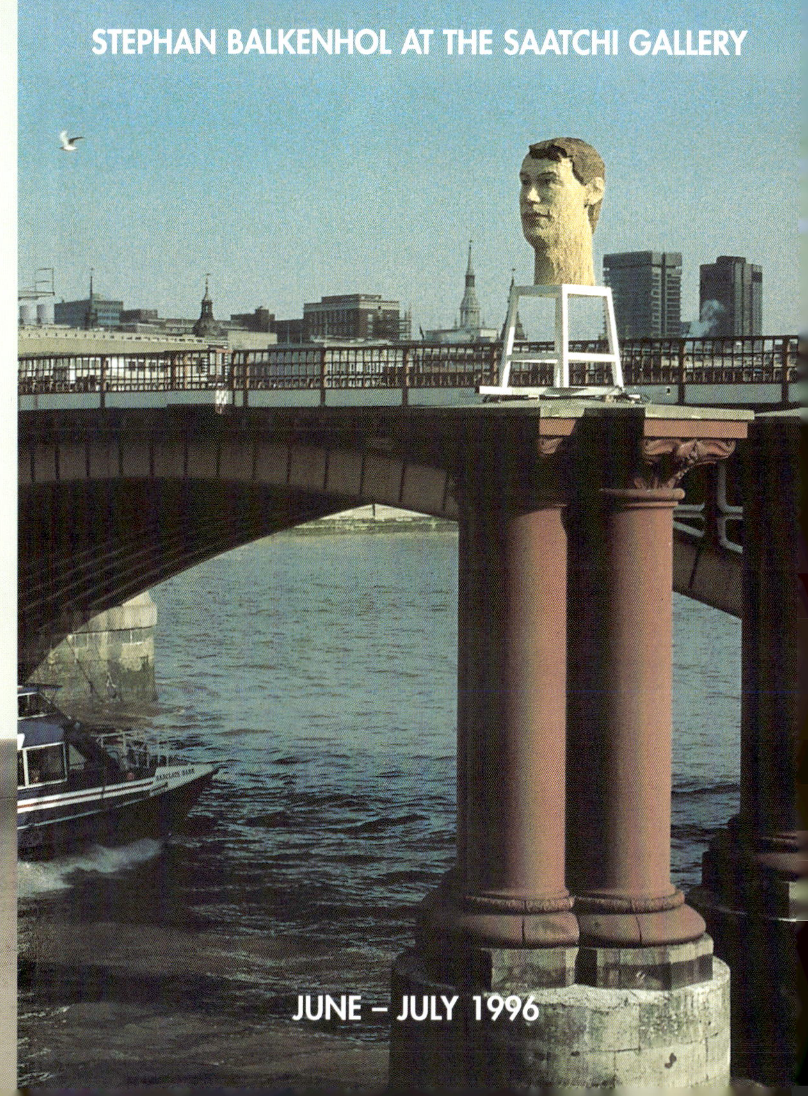

STEPHAN BALKENHOL AT THE SAATCHI GALLERY
JUNE – JULY 1996

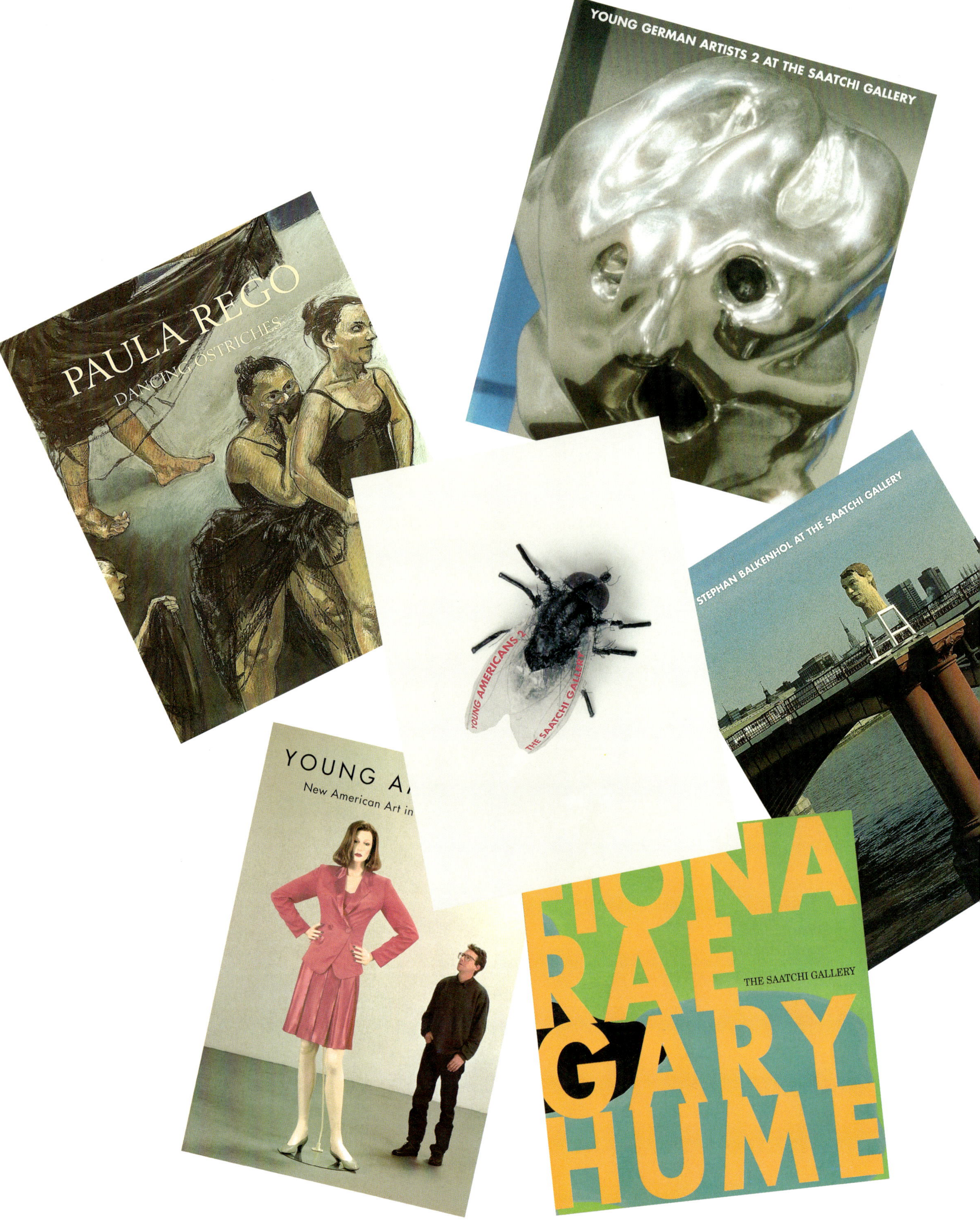

YOUNG GERMAN ARTISTS 2 AT THE SAATCHI GALLERY
PAULA REGO
DANCING OSTRICHES
STEPHAN BALKENHOL AT THE SAATCHI GALLERY
YOUNG AMERICANS 2
THE SAATCHI GALLERY
YOUNG A
New American Art in
FIONA RAE
GARY HUME
THE SAATCHI GALLERY

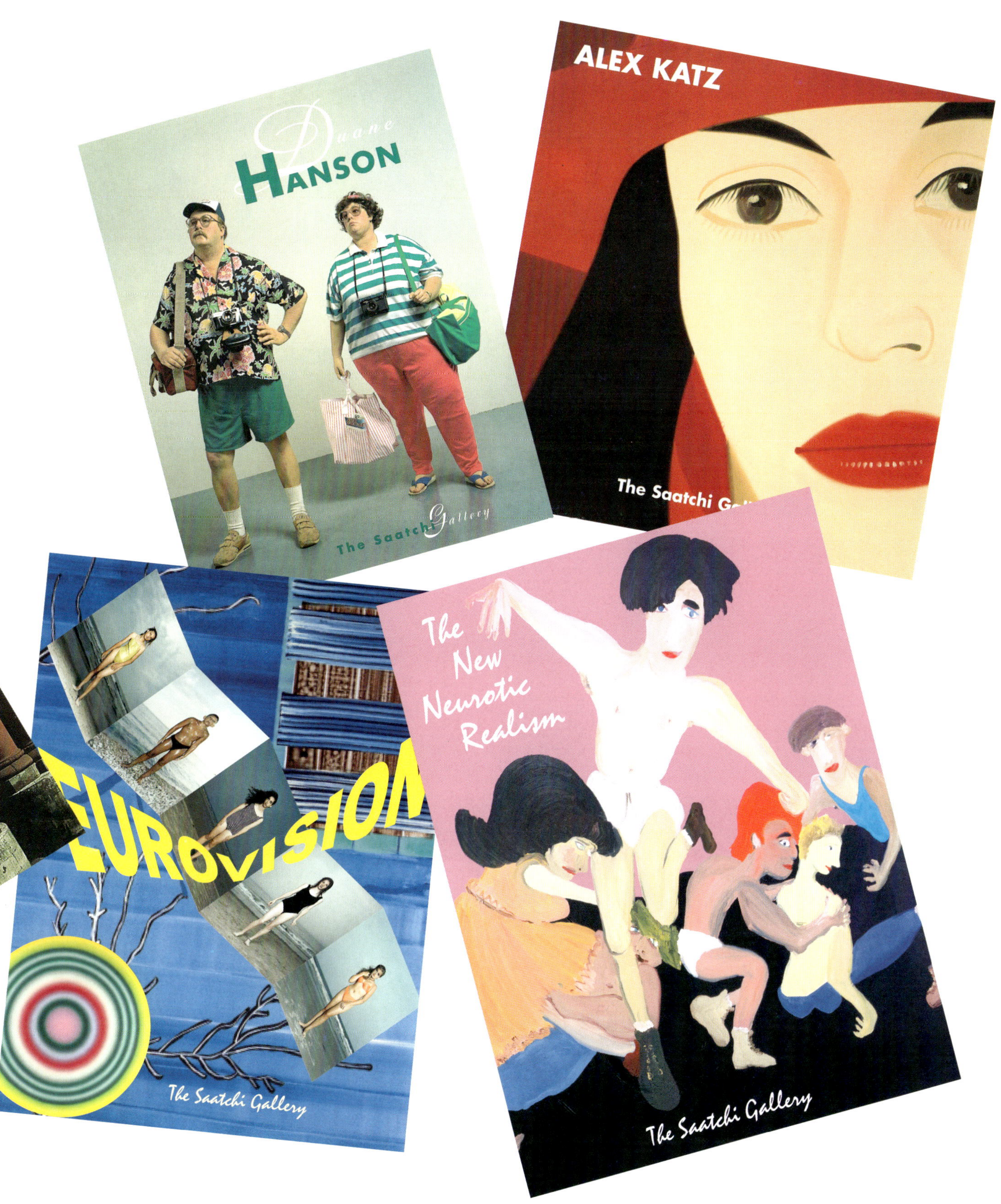

Saatchi Gallery Publications

Distributors: Europe & UK (Cornerhouse) 0161 200 1503 United States: (DAP) From UK 001 732 370 3704
From US 1800 338 2665 Available through major bookstores and museum shops

acknowledgements

we gratefully acknowledge the kind assistance of the artists
and the following individuals and galleries for helping us in
preparing this catalogue:

Galerie Anne de Villepoix, Paris; Galerie Bob van Orsouw,
Zurich; Entwistle Gallery, London; Galerie Hauser & Wirth 2,
Zurich; Irena Hochman Fine Art, New York; Laure Genillard
Gallery, London; Matthew Marks Gallery, New York; The
Photographers' Gallery, London; Galería Soledad Lorenzo,
Madrid; Thomas Healy Gallery, New York; Timothy Taylor
Gallery, London; Victoria Miro Gallery, London and White
Cube Jay Jopling Fine Art, London.

we extend sincere thanks to Patricia Ellis for her essay
EUropium.

we are also grateful to the artists, photographers and
galleries for the use of their photographic material:

Thomas Demand, Rineke Dijkstra, Steven Fuller, Entwistle
Gallery, Giuseppe Gabellone, Galerie Hauser & Wirth 2,
Matthew Hollow, Roberto Marossi, Walter Niedermayr,
Orcutt Van Der Putten and Stephen White.

opposite: Monika Baer *Untitled 1995* oil on canvas 120 x 220 cm
overleaf (1): Giuseppe Gabellone *Tank 1996*
        photographic print 150 x 190 cm
overleaf (2): Walter Niedermayr *Rifugio Auronzo-Le
Cianpedele* (2 parts) *1991-93*
        colour photograph 83 x 208 cm

publications director and curator   Jenny Blyth
assistant curator and registrar   Nigel Hurst
archivist   Linda Copperwheat
press officer   Emma Underhill
gallery assistant   Philippa Adams
installations consultant   Martin McGinn

Monika Baer

1964   Born in Freiburg

EDUCATION
1985-92   Studium an der Kunstakademie Düsseldorf bei Prof. Hüppi
1992   Paris, Stipendium der Kunstakademie Düsseldorf

Lives and works in Düsseldorf

SOLO EXHIBITIONS
1993   Luis Campaña, Cologne
1995   Luis Campaña, Cologne
1997   Le Case D'Arte, Mailand
        Kunsthalle St. Gallen (cat.)
1998   Luis Campaña, Cologne

Giuseppe Gabellone

1973   Born Brindisi, Italy

EDUCATION
1992-94   Academia di Bella Arti, Bologna
1994-97   Academia di Bella Arti, Brera, Milan

Lives and works in Brindisi and Milan

SOLO EXHIBITIONS
1996   Studio Guenzani, Milan
1997   Laure Genillard Gallery, London

Walter Niedermayr

1952   Born in Bolzano, Italy

Lives and works in Bolzano

SOLO EXHIBITIONS
1990   *Architektur; Natur und Technik* Sexten Kultur, Sexten, Italy
        Technische Hochschule Innsbruck; Hochschule für
        Künstlerische und Industrielle Gestaltung, Linz, Austria (cat.)
1992   Rathaus Galerie, Graz, Austria
        Installation dans les gares des lignes Bolzano, Brennero, Italy
        Historische Industriearchitektur Tirol, Südtirol, Vorarlberg
        AR/GE kunst, Bolzano, Taxis Palais, Innsbruck (Austria),
        Museum Bregenz, Austria (cat.)
1993   *Die Bleichen Berge*, AR/GE Kunst Bolzano, Italy (cat.)
1994   *Die Bleichen Berge*, Museum für Gestaltung, Zürich,
        StrumStadtpark, avec Wout Berger, Graz, Austria
        Hotel Café Kusseth, Bolzano, Italy (cat.)
        Libreria-Galeria Einaudi, Milan (cat. Forma)
1995   *Memento*, Haus der Fotografie, Altdorf, Switzerland
1996   Galerie Anne de Villepoix, Paris
        Neue Gesellschaft für Bildenden Kunst, Berlin
        PAUHOF - beobachtet, Galerie im Stifterhaus, Linz, Austria
1997   Galerie Nordenhake, Stockholm
        Kunstverein, Ulm, Germany
        Parco Casse d'espansione del fiume Secchia, Commune di
        Rubiera, Italy
1998   White Cube, London
        Galerie Anne de Villepoix, Paris
        Centre photographique d'île de France, Pontault-Combault
1999   Musée d'Annecy, Annecy
        Robert Miller Gallery, New York

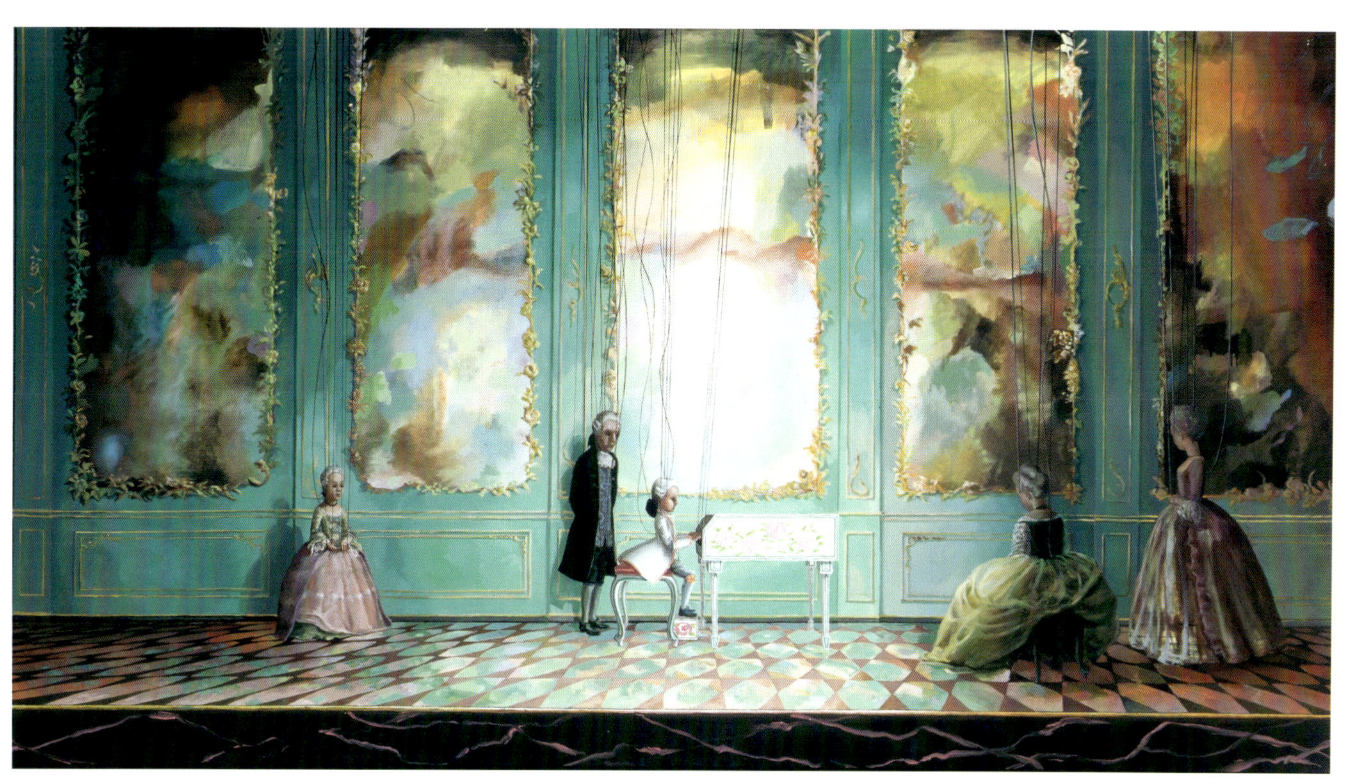

exhibitions held at The Saatchi Gallery

March – October 1985	Donald Judd, Brice Marden, Cy Twombly, Andy Warhol
December 1985 – July 1986	Carl Andre, John Chamberlain, Dan Flavin, Sol Lewitt, Robert Ryman, Frank Stella
September 1986 – July 1987	Anselm Kiefer, Richard Serra
September 1987 – January 1988	'New York Art Now' (Part 1): Ashley Bickerton, Ross Bleckner, Robert Gober, Peter Halley, Jeff Koons, Tim Rollins & K.O.S., Haim Steinbach, Philip Taaffe, Meyer Vaisman
February – April 1988	'New York Art Now' (Part 2): Ashley Bickerton, Carroll Dunham, Robert Gober, Peter Halley, Tishan Hsu, Jon Kessler, Jeff Koons, Allan McCollum, Peter Schuyff, Doug & Mike Starn
April – October 1988	Leon Golub, Philip Guston, Sigmar Polke, Joel Shapiro
November 1988 – April 1989	Jennifer Bartlett, Eric Fischl, Elizabeth Murray, Susan Rothenberg
April – October 1989	Robert Mangold, Bruce Nauman
November 1989 – February 1990	Leon Kossoff, Bill Woodrow
March – November 1990	Frank Auerbach, Lucian Freud, Richard Deacon
January – July 1991	Richard Artschwager, Cindy Sherman, Richard Wilson
September 1991 – February 1992	Mike Bidlo, Manuel Ocampo, Andres Serrano
March – October 1992	'Young British Artists I': John Greenwood, Damien Hirst, Alex Landrum, Langlands & Bell, Rachel Whiteread
October – December 1992	'Out of Africa': Contemporary African artists from the Pigozzi Collection
February – July 1993	'Young British Artists II': Rose Finn-Kelcey, Sarah Lucas, Marc Quinn, Mark Wallinger
September – December 1993	'American Art in the 20th Century' presented by The Royal Academy of Arts, London
February – July 1994	'Young British Artists III': Simon Callery, Simon English, Jenny Saville
September 1994	'A Positive View' 20th Century International Photography presented by Vogue
November 1994 – February 1995	Paula Rego, John Murphy, Avis Newman
April 1995 – June 1995	'Young British Artists IV': John Frankland, Marcus Harvey, Brad Lochore, Marcus Taylor, Gavin Turk
September – December 1995	'Young British Artists V': Glenn Brown, Keith Coventry, Hadrian Pigott, Kerry Stewart
January – May 1996	'Young Americans': Janine Antoni, Gregory Green, Jacqueline Humphries, Sean Landers, Charles Long, Tony Oursler, Richard Prince, Charles Ray, Kiki Smith
June – July 1996	'Stephan Balkenhol' Sculptures 1988 –1996
September – December 1996	'Young British Artists VI': Jordan Baseman, Daniel Coombs, Claude Heath, John Isaacs, Nina Saunders
January – April 1997	Fiona Rae and Gary Hume
April – August 1997	Duane Hanson
September – December 1997	'Young German Artists 2': Thomas Grünfeld, Andreas Gursky, Stefan Hablützel, Martin Honert, Thomas Ruff, Thomas Schütte
January – April 1998	Alex Katz 'Twenty Five Years of Painting'
April – July 1998	'Young Americans 2' Part One: Ashley Bickerton, Carroll Dunham, David Salle, Jessica Stockholder, Terry Winters
September – November 1998	'Young Americans 2' Part Two: Michael Ashkin, John Currin, Tom Friedman, Martin Kersels, Clay Ketter, Robin Lowe, Josiah McElheny, Sarah Morris, Laura Owens, Elizabeth Peyton, Monique Prieto, Brian Tolle, Sue Williams, Lisa Yuskavage
January – March 1999	'Neurotic Realism' Part One: Stephen Gontarski, Brian Griffiths, Martin Maloney, Paul Smith, Tomoko Takahashi

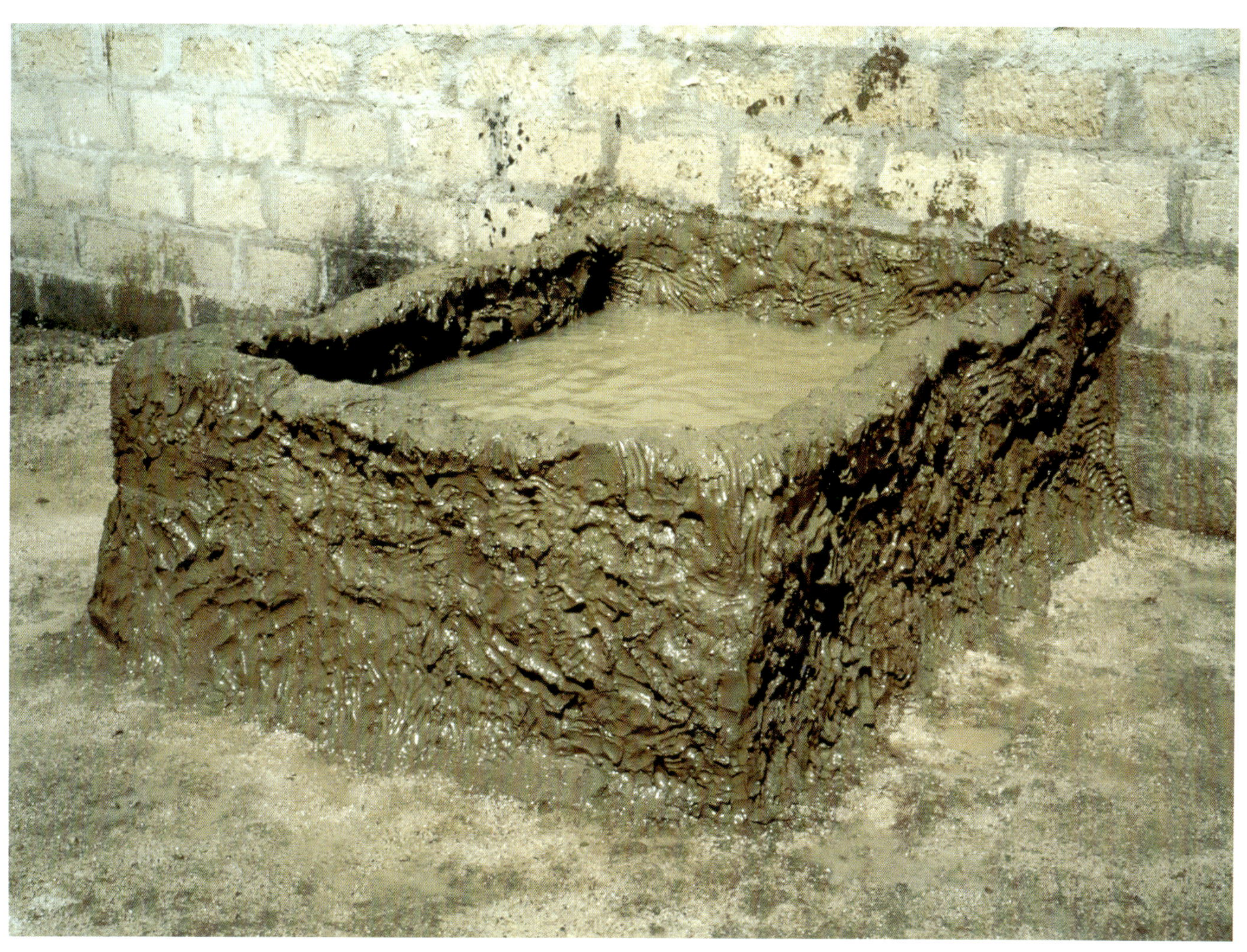

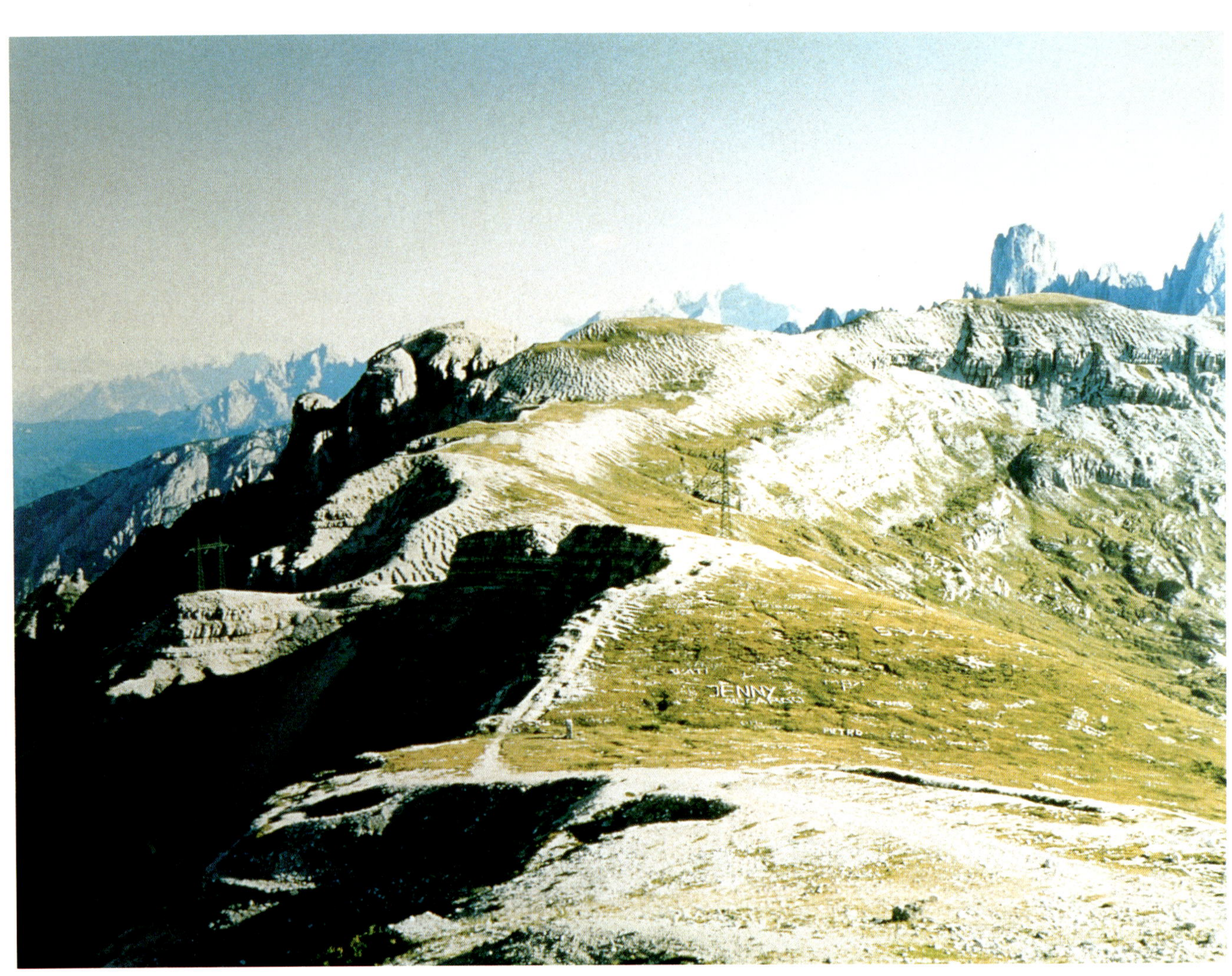
JENNY
PETRO

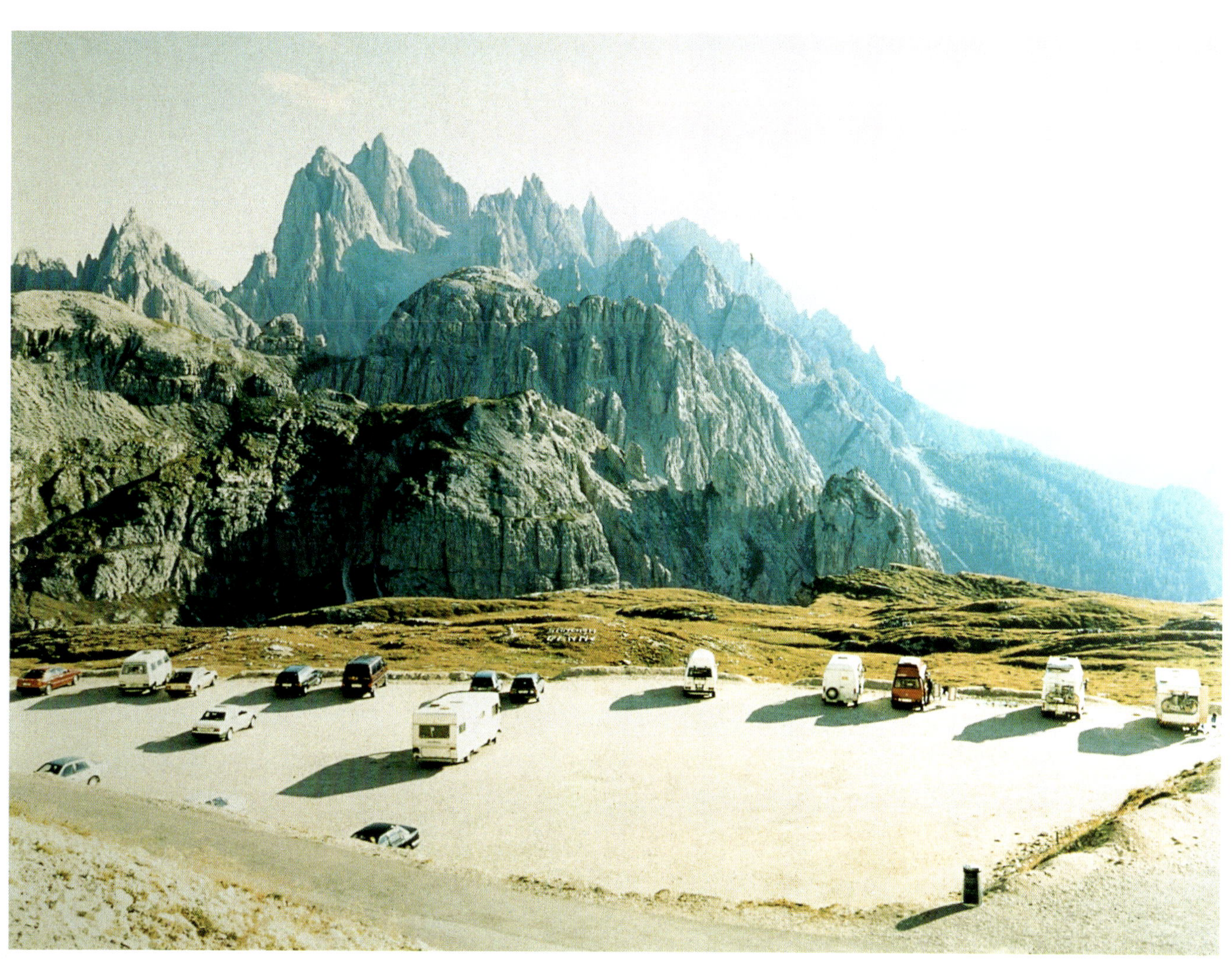

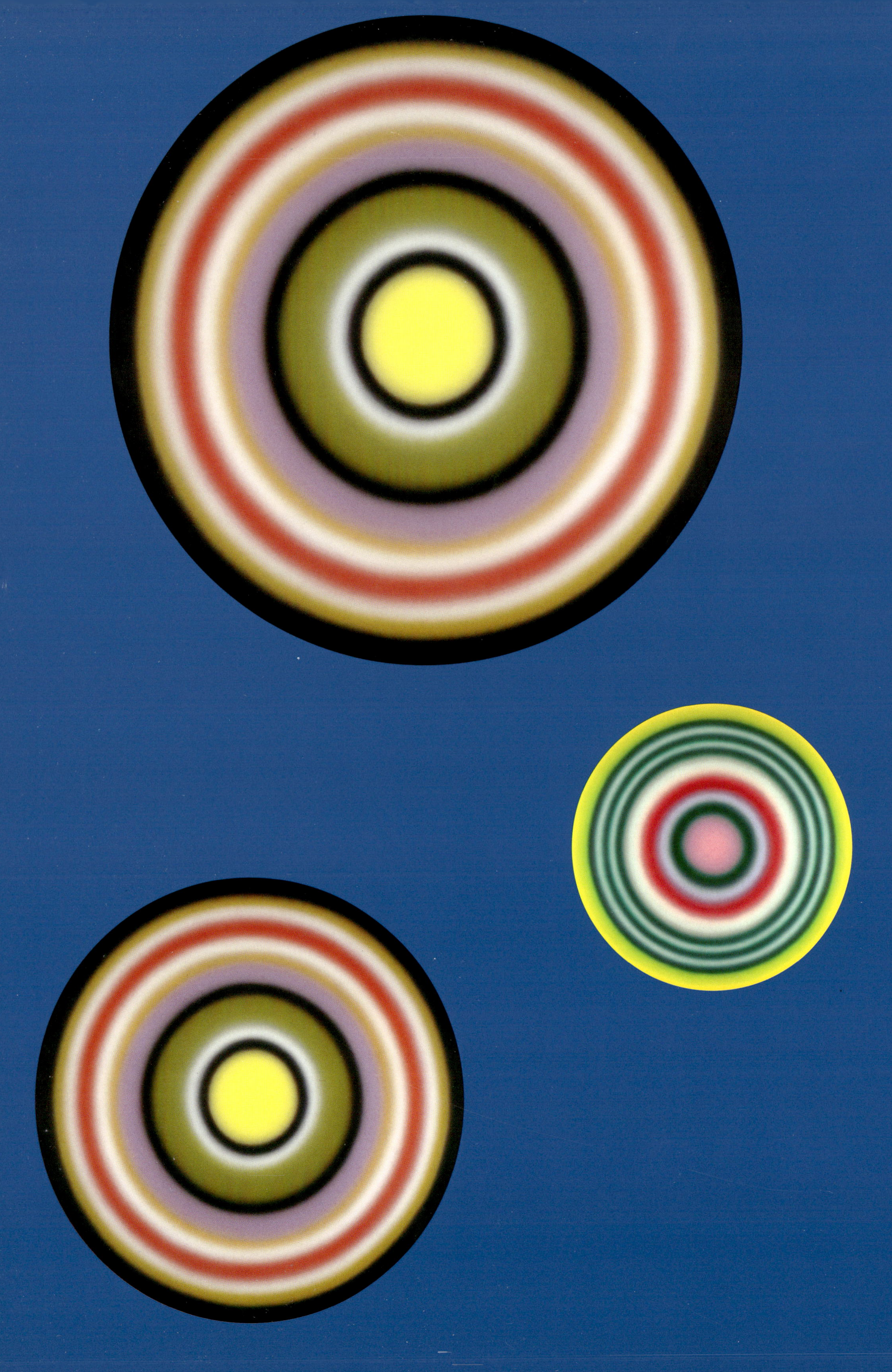